TRANSFORMED

AN EVOLUTION OF MIND, BODY AND SPIRIT:

MY JOURNEY OF LOSING WEIGHT AND GAINING A NEW LIFE

Authored By

Nia Danielle

TRANSFORMED

All Rights Reserved.

No part of this book may be used or reproduced by any means, graphic, electronic, or mechanical, including photocopying, or by any information storage retrieval system without the written permission of the owner except in the case of brief quotations in articles and reviews.

Printed in the United States of America

THIS BOOK IS NOT INTENDED TO BE A HISTORY TEXT. While every effort has been made to check the accuracy of dates, locations, and historical information, no claims are made as to the accuracy of such information.

Book category: Self-help

Cover, author and after photos: Nvision Photography

For author appearances and interviews, contact author:

bookings@tru4me.com or call 404-475-2523

Copyright © 2024 by Tru4Me LLC

ISBN: 979-8-9909297-0-8

DEDICATION

This book, as well as all that I am and ever hope to be is dedicated to the two beings who had a tremendous hand in who I am today. My mom, Carmen, and my grandmother, Danna Lee. There are not enough words to express my love and gratitude to you both. I am covered daily by you Mamma, from the ancestral realm, and by you Mommy. May you both continue to bless and guide me always. I love you.

ACKNOWLEDGEMENTS

I would like to thank God/Goddess for being with me and showing up for me literally to let me know I am loved, and my life truly has meaning. To my parents, Carmen and William, thank you for agreeing to be the catalyst through which I arrived here and provided me with the best of you both. I will love and honor you always.

To my brother, Haneef, thank you for being there for me since you arrived on this planet. You have loved, supported, and taken a lot of the brunt and backlash from my countless attempts at dieting. You have been my coach and have been fired so many times, I cannot count, just to turn around and do it all over again. I could not have chosen a better sibling to go through this journey with and I am honored to be your sister. I love you more than words, brother.

Martina, you have been there since my arrival in Georgia, and we have laughed, fought, and loved like sisters. Thank you for always being there and for all the guidance you provided throughout the process of creating this book. I could not have done it without your help and expertise. Love you Capricorn sister.

Adriane, the big sister I never knew I needed until we found each other. You have encouraged me to be the very best version of myself and never allowed me to settle for less. Thank you for being there to gently, and not-so gently nudge me in the right direction and start me on my physical fitness journey. I love you so much, you are my person.

Nzingha, throughout the years, you have encouraged me to love myself, understand my worth, and comforted me through some of the most difficult times of my life. You cried and prayed with me, and you were the first ever manifestation partner I had, I love and thank you, sister, from another mister.

Sophia, you encouraged me and remained steadfast with me in my fitness journey even though you are light years ahead of me. You have been patient and encouraging and most importantly, made me accountable to show up for myself and trust the process. I appreciate you so much, fam.

Sabina, you were there from the very beginning of my creation of this book. You took the time to go on a retreat to help me record what I emotionally could not write down at the time. You held space and helped me to form what has now become an official book. Thanks so much for my December birthday sis.

To my baby cousin Deshawna, over the past two years you have provided the emotional support and encouragement I needed to forge ahead with the confidence that I know what I know, and that I am ready to help others. I love you, my birthday twin.

TRANSFORMED

While I could spend the next 10 pages thanking everyone who has had a positive impact on my life, for the sake of time and space, I will have to limit it to just a few. But know that if you indeed had a positive interaction with me that helped me to get to the place in my life that I am now, I am grateful for you. **Thank You All.**

CHAPTER 1

Why Go Public?

Many people will probably speculate why I am writing this book and putting my business out there. I have trepidation about writing this book because there will be some critics who will ridicule me as they will believe I am promoting cutting your body, or certain spiritual practices that I will speak about in the coming chapters. I would have to admit, yes, I am nervous about some of the backlash that might come, not only from strangers but from people within my circle. However, as old folks say, "My soul is settled" so I know it's time and I am ready for wherever this mission is choosing to take me next.

When I was a little girl, I had fantasies of how my life would unfold, envisioning what I wanted to be when I grew up, how I would look, who I wanted to marry, and most importantly, how freaking extravagant that wedding was going to be!

But for me what I envisioned for myself didn't happen that way. Events occurred that brought about a mental and emotional weight which then manifested into physical weight. By the time I realized what was happening, I was so depressed, despondent, angry, and obese with no real guide to getting out of the hole I was in, that it seemed completely hopeless.

People had all kinds of advice for me at that time and a little bit of shaming to go along with it. Some of the advice or guidance I received were things like, "Since I put it on naturally, I needed to take it off naturally." Or "Just step away from the table, you need to have more self-control," and "You need to exercise, you are not really trying hard enough, other people are doing it, so can you." That led to a cycle of yo-yo dieting, starvation, self-deprecation and a laundry list of pills, teas, and other "diet aids" that were unhealthy both physically and mentally.

Once I made the decision to go the weight loss surgery route, I realized there was a shame in that as well. No one wanted to talk about it if they did do it and many people shamed folks from wanting to go through the process because it was the "easy way out". Let me tell you, there wasn't anything easy about this journey, the very process for approval alone is rigorous, which I will get into later in this book.

TRANSFORMED

Making the decision to have weight loss surgery has absolutely changed my life and given me a new path to follow that has exceeded the dreams I had as a child. Plus, this is not just about physical weight, this journey was emotional and spiritual as I learned are all tied together. I had to be willing to go the distance and confront the demons in my life to elevate myself to the life I deserved.

Before you go any further into this book, I want to put on the record that this is **MY STORY**. The events that occurred and the outcome are all my experiences, and they may not resonate with you and that is fine. I'm not here to win everyone over to follow the blueprint of what I did to achieve my goals, I am just here to provide another perspective and alternative. My Grandmother always said, "There was more than one way to get to ten," this book provides another route.

This road was not easy, and I am sure it hasn't been easy for whoever is led to pick up this book and read it, but it can be done.

I do have a few disclaimers; the weight loss journey part of this book may not be for everyone as there are so many people out there who are happy in their skin, the way they are… if this is you then I am not sharing this for you. I am so glad for you truly! I'm talking to the people who are not at peace with their weight for either aesthetic or medical reasons and want or need to do something about it to possibly save their lives or change the quality of their lives for the better.

The second disclaimer is that if the weight loss journey is not your story, it may be someone else's that you know and you might see yourself as one of the people in my journey. Everyone needs a support system, so if that is you, this book might help you understand the person in your life's struggle which will help you be more of a positive influence and provide a soft place to fall if they do stumble from time to time along the way.

Also, my journey doesn't just contain weight issues, it contains a host of other challenges that life may bring emotionally, physically, and spiritually. Therefore, anyone reading this book may read about an experience I've gone through, and it may resonate with what you have experienced in your life and have come out on the other side victorious.

So, putting my story out there, the good, bad, and ugly will help even one person to understand that they are not alone, there are people who may not have the same story, but the outcome is the same, and are inspired by my journey so far to start the path to change theirs, well this is all worth it.

Let Us Begin...

CHAPTER 2

Let's Begin At The Beginning

I had to fight to be here.

Well not me personally, but my mom. She fought hard to make sure I was brought into this world because there were people that didn't want me here and that energy influences the person growing inside the womb. My origin story started where I was not wanted so I carried a lesson of unworthiness into this life's journey. This resulted in ushering in a need to prove myself and please people simply because I wasn't welcomed into this plane of existence. What we forget is that everything, and I do mean everything, is designed to move your needle along on the Soul's journey in your incarnation.

Now, like I said in the last chapter, this book is not for everybody. This book is for those who can benefit from it, so if it is not for you, pass it on to somebody whom you feel will benefit from the knowledge I will be sharing and if not put it back on the shelf as I am a Capricorn and part of Gen X, so I'm not easily offended!

TRANSFORMED

I'm not going to get deep into my family history, nor will I tell you my entire life story, this ain't a memoir, consider the first few chapters as a highlights reel (y'all don't need to know all my business, quit being nosey!).

My family and key people will come up in the story, of course, to assist in laying the foundation of situations that occurred and had a major impact on my life, but I probably won't use any names outside of my mom, grandmother, brother and maybe some friends who were integral parts of my support system. This is to protect; I don't want to say the guilty but just to protect the people who may not have been aware of what they were doing. But also, I will change the names of some real-life "villains" as I don't want them to get the slightest recognition from this book… or 15 minutes of fame for you off my pain. However, if you recognize yourself in some of these people, cool, now you know, and if you know better, you can do better.

I was born in a log cabin…nah…I'm just kidding, I wanted to see if you were paying attention, plus, did you check the cover, I ain't that old! I was born in the inner city of Newark, New Jersey to two young teen parents.

My mom was seventeen and a true Jersey girl, originally from a well-to-do neighborhood in Newark, who went to catholic school and all that jazz. This was her life until my grandparents split up and my grandmother had to move to the inner city and later the projects with six children while my grandfather went on to live the high life with his new wife. There are a lot of traumas with that story but that is not my story to expose, just understand there is such a thing as Karma, and no one is exempt from receiving that karma, good or bad.

My dad was eighteen and originally from High Point, North Carolina, and his mom relocated him and his five younger siblings to a Newark project. I'm not sure about my dad's life prior to coming to New Jersey, but I do know he never knew his dad and was my grandma's support system in taking care of her children, which ultimately led to a life of dreams unfulfilled. I am a firm believer in that, so in other words…I said what I said.

 My parents were young, in love, and totally clueless on how to raise kids but they really wanted one, both, I believe, stemming from what was missing in their lives, and wanted to build a family that they defined. But hurt and trauma are not good building blocks for the family they were trying to create at such a young age, but they tried and were married for a couple of months after I was born on Valentine's Day.

I was brought into a family with a lot of religious beliefs! My dad's people were Methodist and on my mom's side, my grandmother's people were Catholic, and my grandfather's side was Baptist. Jeesh!

When you think about it, that is a whole lot of Catechisms and fried fish dinner plates!

When I finally got here, of course, the tune changed, and everybody forgot that initial conflict. I was there, the very first grandchild on both sides of the family. I was doted on, and it did help that I was sooo cute! I was a very well-behaved child, loving, outgoing, smart, well-mannered and, did I mention adorable! It seemed like despite my shaky beginnings; I had the makings of a charmed life. Then tragedy struck a week after my second birthday. I was hit by a drunk driver as I was running out into the street to retrieve a ball. Back in the 70's, cars were made with real iron so you can imagine that grill hitting my face.

According to those who remember, because of course, I don't have any recollection whatsoever of this accident, the car hit me so hard it knocked out my front teeth and gums, broke my jaw, broke a blood vessel in my left eye, damaged my cheek and my upper jaw permanently, and I had a hole in my chin. I still have a visible scar underneath my bottom lip, and I lost both my baby teeth and adult teeth as a result of it, so I still bear the marks of that accident both physically and up until this point emotionally.

The doctors stated if he was driving a little faster, I would've died instantly. It is safe to assume an impact like that would likely affect my cognitive development, but according to my mother and my grandmother, it seemed that I got smarter post-accident. I cannot imagine what my mom went through emotionally seeing her only child at the time in that state. I've heard the stories of my mom, my mom's mother who I called grandma up until that point but after the accident, all I could call out was Mamma and my step grandmother MaMa was about to be thrown out of the hospital because they were causing such a raucous. But I can't blame them, and I also understand why my mom was so strict about who my brother and I later stayed with, because she let me spend the night with other people against her better judgment when it happened.

Even with all those scars, I was still the same cute, bubbly little girl, "true beauty like mine, is never taken away, no matter what is done to it." That is a direct quote from my mom, and I love her for it. Do I blame my mom for what happened? Hell No! Looking back at the fact she didn't want to let me stay and I cried to stay, which was the only reason she acquiesced, I know now that it was my soul that knew what was to happen had to happen to be a catalyst for what the journey of my life would be. We agreed to this before I came to this earthly plane and I did what I could as a two-year-old and she ignored what the old folks call "her first mind", to ensure it happened. I commend us both for our courage.

Remember I said, the energy that surrounds you coming into this world will follow you and it might be that overall arc that you need to overcome. Again, mine was a feeling of worthiness and I remember saying the same prayer every night, "Now, I lay me down to sleep..." and I ended it with, "And make me a very nice, good little girl, Amen." I was unaware that I was literally chanting a mantra. Of course, I didn't know I was chanting a mantra or what that even was at that time but that was indeed a mantra. The mantra itself is not damaging in any way, but if you couple that with a feeling of unworthiness, and a need to be accepted not as who I was or wanted to be but who I thought other people wanted me to be, that is a recipe for a very unfulfilling and inauthentic existence.

I was raised Catholic (my mom's mother's side won) and went to parochial school nearly my entire school career, from kindergarten through tenth grade, but I had the experience growing up with all three of those religious practices. If I'm to be perfectly honest, that is a lot of strict, controlling, and fear-mongering tactics to imbed in an impressionable child who took everything at face value. Now, do I practice any of those religions? No. Do I regret being in those or any of the other sectors of Christianity that would come later? No. Each religious practice that I was exposed to, especially Catholicism and Charismatic faith, gave me the building blocks that led to the spiritual practices I implemented in my life today. But we will get more into that later. Plus, alongside these religious beliefs was an undercurrent of practices that popped up in a lot of black families. Using certain herbs to cure certain things or doing certain practices like banking or cleaning at certain times. These little gems, which I was more fascinated with than anything else I was being taught played a major role in my spiritual quest.

This is a trinity story, as all things divine happen in three: body, soul, and spirit. I've discussed my spiritual and soul foundations, so let's discuss the physical aspect of my journey, not just the results of the car accident but the way I was taught to view my body early. We are taught to see ourselves by the people around us, the ones that we look up to the most, or it could come from a random but very impactful experience. Mine came from both.

There may be some children who had an opportunity to look into the mirror and explore their bodies and what they look like and define for themselves what is their version of beauty and self-acceptance. I, like many others, did not have that experience. My very first experience of self-awareness about the skin I was in came from a random little girl when I was a little over three years old.

Storytime:

I was around three when my mom, dad, and I were living on the Marine base in South Carolina as my dad had joined the service. As young as I was, I remember this like it just happened, I was outside playing alone in the sand not too far from our trailer. My mom was inside because back in those days, especially on-base housing, children could go outside and be safe. I was outside making hand sand dunes like a normal kid, when a little white girl, a few years older than me who also lived on the base, was riding her bike straight toward me. I looked up and as she was barreling toward me, she yelled out, "Move nigger!" Now, I was not sure what that word meant but the way she said it and what it made me feel along with the fact she just tried to run me over sent me running into the house.

I remember my mom asking me what was wrong, and me relaying the events that led up to my flight. After that, it was a blur of my mom in a frenzy, running to try to break into the trailer of the girl who lived there to beat the hell out of her mom who was the source of that nurtured racism. My mom is a 20-year-old Scorpio from Newark, NJ who has fought multiple people at one time. Needless to say, her heart don't pump no Kool-Aid okay!

A couple of friends she had at the time living there had to hold her back while my dad was summoned from the base to come try to calm her down. That encounter had an impact on me as that was my first experience with racism and that I was "different" and therefore not liked, not because of anything I did but simply because of the skin in which I was born. I weep for the loss of my innocence at such an early age and the countless other melanin babies who've had to deal with this issue before and after me.

The next incident that I can recall, which made me very aware of what body image was and what that means personally, involved a very important person in my life who provided the catalyst for a very painful journey in my perception of my own beauty.

Disclaimer:

Before I get deeper into the story or any of the stories that will come after this, I want to make one thing crystal clear, I know for a fact that the family members that I have did the things that they did not out of malice but out of fear and love. They knew they wanted to guide me to make me the best person that I could be but back then at that time and even up to today, we as a melanite community tend to operate out of fear-based love. We fear what may or may not happen to our children, so we raise them with certain fears or implant certain beliefs into them like inadvertently body shaming our kids or oversexualizing our kids because we are over-sexualized as people of color, so I get it.

So, I want to make this very clear that I hold nothing against my family. I absolutely love each one of my family members, with emphasis on Family and not relatives which are two very different things to me, but the ones in this story I absolutely know in my heart that each of them had my best interest at heart, they just didn't go about it the way that would have been the healthiest for me.

Plus, I know that each of us agreed to play our roles in guiding the direction my life needed to take to fulfill my purpose, including me. My mom said as a very young toddler, I would say I was going to be fat just like my grandma (my dad's mom), so my soul knew the path that was set for me to travel.

In other words, allow grace and space for my family, please, and thank you.

Let's proceed, shall we?

I was six -years old when I was sent to Georgia for the summer to visit family. Mamma came down with my brother and cousin to spend the last weeks of the summer and then brought us all back home. At the end of the trip, I remember getting dressed to leave for the bus station and about to head back "up north." She looked at me and said, "Oh we gotta watch you because you are getting kind of plump there, look at that belly!" Up until that point, I had no self-awareness of how or what I looked like body-wise, and I had no concept of what is or isn't aesthetically pleasing.

I can't even really describe to you what that's like unless you can go back into your mind's eye and remember that time or point in your life when you as a child just had zero awareness about what was acceptable or unacceptable, you just were. I do remember at that moment that I realized that I have a body, but this body is not "right." There is something wrong with this body and I need to fix it but not quite sure about how I should go about fixing it.

I'm approaching this, of course from the mind of a six-year-old. All I know is that someone whom I admire so much, and who was very much as close to God as you can get on earth aside from my Mom was telling me that there was something wrong, so I knew that I needed to fix it and in that moment, I birthed a feeling of, " I'm not good enough," the way that I am and that there is something wrong with me.

I remember around that time back home in Newark, I was still six years old when I had a sleepover with a friend of mine who was a classmate and her older sister who was about twelve and I was molested by this girl. She touched me, and she had both her sister and I touch each other. I remember feeling uncomfortable. I remember feeling that this was not right, but I complied.

Looking back on that, I think the reason behind me, and my compliance was that she was older, and I was always told to do what my elders told me to do, and she was "in charge" because she was older. This was the first time that I experienced sexual assault. A violation happened to me that was unwarranted, and I felt powerless to stop it. I didn't know how to even tell someone about it because I didn't even know what it was that happened, I just knew I didn't like the way it made me feel.

Later down the line, when I was in therapy about a myriad of things during the course of my weight loss journey, I realized that we give away our children's power when we make them hug and kiss people that they don't want to share intimacy with. We tell them that how they feel about their bodies doesn't matter, and it's more about what the other person wants. That it's better to make that other person feel better than for them to feel good about themselves. Think about how many times we've seen a child being forced and threatened to embrace someone when they clearly don't want to, despite the body language they display during and after.

So, if this is the only takeaway that you have from this book, if you have children or children are in your life, please do not take their power or their autonomy away from them. When you do that, it puts them in danger of being prey to someone abusing them and they in turn feel as if there is no recourse because they have zero power in the situation. I'm not saying that will always happen, however, it does put one in the mindset of," I really don't have autonomy over myself, and I have to sacrifice how I feel for someone else's happiness," and that's not a good way to approach life, as this can lead to some very toxic relationships as an adult.

Not too long after that incident occurred, I was invited to spend the night at one of my uncle's girlfriend's house, she also had a daughter who was around twelve years old and I do recall now that the two girls were friends, so I guess a conversation must have been had

TRANSFORMED

about what happened because during the course of this sleepover she tried the same exact thing.

Fortunately, I have no idea why this happened but at the same time, I know why this happened, divine intervention, and timing. My uncle came into the room at the precise moment things were about to take a turn for the worse and flipped on the light and yelled, "What are you doing with your arm around her?!" Get off her like that and turn your backs to one another!"

He walked out and kept the door open and the light on for the rest of the night, peeking in often. I never slept over at that place again and after that, I never had another sleepover with anybody unless they were family.

He saved me that night and later I found out maybe where his spidey sense came from, but it's not my place to tell his story, I'm just grateful that he was there to save me from what was about to happen.

I'm not sure if he told anybody about that night. If he told my mother or my grandmother no one would ever say anything to me but then again, I was six, so what would they have said? I never told my mom or anybody what had happened prior to him coming into the room or what had happened at my own sleepover a few weeks before. I don't think I talked about those incidents at all for at least a good 30 years, simply for the fact that I had very mixed feelings about what occurred. Not just from the molestation part but from the fact that it was females, so I struggled a lot with that aspect for quite some time.

I wasn't sure if it was something that they saw in me and later down the line I was torn as to whether that was part of my sexual orientation. Not that there is anything wrong with being LGBTQ nor am I saying that being molested leads to being gay because it absolutely doesn't! One has zero to do with the other but in the future, as an adolescent and teen, when I thought back on it, I just wasn't sure if it was the reason why they felt they could do the things they did to me. Hell, I wasn't even sure that was who they were or if they even knew exactly what they were doing or why they did what they did.

At the end of the day, it doesn't even matter why they chose me, it could have been completely random, or I could have been targeted, it doesn't matter, what matters most is knowing it was not my fault and there was nothing I did or didn't do that could place blame or shame at my feet, nor does it define who I am.

Of course, these epiphanies will come many years and many pounds later.

Gentle Reminder:

During this time, we were living in the projects, but I was also going to a private Catholic school. I was gifted in reading, writing and I had a great imagination. I wrote poetry and short stories. I competed in oratory competitions. I had mostly straight A's except for math which were B's but then later in high school, they became less than that because when you start adding letters to numbers…yeah you lost me. I had dreams of becoming a singer, actress, and dancer since I could remember and was always confused when folks laughed at that revelation. Being a star was just as normal to me as becoming a teacher or a fireman.

All in all, my childhood consisted of the normal happenings of black kids growing up in the Gen X era, great birthdays, Christmases, cookouts, and family Sunday dinners. Trick-or-treating in the suburbs where there was good candy, roller rinks, block parties, and courtyard parties in the PJ's. Concerts in the park, penny candy, coming in before the streetlights came on, and of course there was our fair share of family drama and violence that you experience growing up in the inner city. I wanted to interject this just in case you all forgot this is not a memoir, so there are so many great memories and tragic histories that are not present because they are not relevant to my self-image and the journey but of course, all my history has contributed to my overall self-actualization. Again, this book contains highlights, there are so many parts of my life that were normal-ish.

Moving on:

By the time I was around eight, most of my immediate family members were out of the projects. My mom had moved my brother and I to East Orange, New Jersey. My parents broke up shortly after my brother was conceived. My dad still resided in New Jersey, but he was not a permanent fixture in our lives. I know that some people are not going to like to see that in writing but if you remember correctly, you know that is the truth. I do know that my father was dealing with a lot of demons in his life, which may have influenced the way he parented especially since he didn't know his own father to the day that he died, so I don't hold any grudges and we will get more into our story soon.

The group of apartment buildings we lived in was very much like a community, a little U-shape community of buildings with a lot of single moms working multiple jobs and raising kids. The superintendent was like Bookman from Good Times. There was an assistant superintendent, let's just call him Chester. Chester was one of those dudes who always had candy and loose change in his pockets to hand to the kids as soon as we saw him. The kids loved him, and as soon as he came around, they yelled out his name, Chester! Chester, give me candy! Give me a quarter! He always acted like we were bothering him but would be digging in his pockets and at the same time fussing at us to get away. The parents, especially the single moms, looked out for him because he would give extensions on the rent when needed or watch out for us kids. It was nothing to see a child deliver a plate of food or be sent to his apartment to see if he needed anything from the store because we were making a run.

Around this time, I was like nine or ten years old, and I was about 5'3, almost as tall as I'm going to get right now which is 5' 5, and pretty stacked at around 115 pounds. I bloomed early as a child. I remember wearing my first training bra when I was in the third grade, and I got my cycle when I was 9 so I developed much faster than my family was accustomed to back in those days. I don't think my family knew how to deal with that outside of being fearful that if I was maturing this fast, I would eventually 'blow up' which was the going consensus.

I always heard, "If you keep eating the way you're eating, you are going to be fat." You're going to be fat like your dad's people, or you're going to be fat like this person or that person, as they pointed out random heavy-set people on the street.

That took a toll on how I viewed myself and the perception of how some of my family members viewed me because later I was talking to my brother and he said, "You know looking back at these pictures, you weren't fat, you weren't big at all. You were big to me then, because when I remember you in my mind's eye you've always been big."

I also remember telling a good friend of mine that I couldn't wear a certain item of clothing because I was "too fat." She asked me how that could be when we were the same height and weight. I acknowledged that she wasn't fat, but I was.

That is the persuasive power of perception. How you project to small children will have a huge influence on the way a child perceives themselves and the world around them. You must have that responsibility to know that you are shaping a person's worldview. You are helping to shape how they feel about themselves, how they want to present themselves to others in the world, and how they view others in this world.

That is how important parenting truly is... You are literally shaping the future.

Also, I didn't realize this until later when I began my journey of manifestation, affirmation, visualization, etc., that words are powerful, words speak life or death, and you are manifesting the things that you are saying if the feeling is strong enough. So, the very fact that they were fearful of me being overweight manifested in me literally. The fear of becoming fat became a driving force in my life. It became an all-consuming thought monster that always loomed in the back of my head.

I recall I was sent over to an aunt's house on some weekends or during a winter or spring break when I was around eleven, where she created a sort of "fat camp" in which there was a timer to alert us to drink water every hour. We ate two salads a day and then a healthy meal for dinner. Then, every night we exercised in her living room. I began to call her "Auntie diet" in my head from that point on. My weight was a collective issue for all the adults in my life and they began to separate me from the rest of the kids by not allowing me to have snacks at times when my cousins and my brother would be allowed. This was around the time the sparks of anger and resentment began to burn in my wee bitty soul.

Let's get back to the story, shall we?

Chester, the assistant superintendent, happened to live in our building, on the second floor, and we lived on the floor above him. Of course, we know words like 'grooming' now but back then in the '80s no one used the term and discussed molestation or sexual assault outside of the, "if someone touches you, you tell us, and we will kill them." Impassioned speeches, it wasn't really discussed. As a matter of fact, in the black community, we are very slow to discuss these things, or if we do it's in whispered tones, especially if there are known pedophiles in your family.

We seem to just steer our young girls or boys away from them under the disguise of "we don't let the kids stay alone with this person or that person but never actually do anything about it.

In many instances, when situations are discovered, the blame will fall on the child involved versus putting the accountability on the assailant and prosecuting them. We need to end the 'what goes on in this house stays in this house' family mentality and start speaking up for our loved ones, the victims, so we can begin to heal this trauma.

Well, Chester began grooming me with little gestures. At first, he was just paying a little more attention to me than he did the other children and giving me dollars instead of quarters. Then, he upped the stakes and began to give me fives and tens and then later twenties. He gave me extra candy then it started to escalate more when he knew I was home alone if there was no school that day or if I was out sick. He would then slide adult magazines under the door because, of course, we were not allowed to open a door for anybody, not even family members.

I had to hide the large amounts of money that I was accumulating from him in my drawer, and I was almost busted one time when my mom went into my drawer to get something. She was like, "Where in the hell did you get all this money?!" I said, "Oh no, it's one of my friends. I'm holding it for her for a surprise gift for her mom."

TRANSFORMED

She said, "Well make sure you take that and give it back tomorrow." After that, I had to move my hiding place.

Things became progressively worse, and he started to make lewd comments and sexual advances by trying to look underneath my uniform skirt dress when I ascended the steps to our apartment. I felt so uncomfortable that I started wearing shorts under the skirt. I dreaded having to go downstairs to ask if he wanted anything from the store. I started to try to avoid him as best I could, but he always seemed to know when I was coming out of my apartment. I know some folks are asking themselves why I didn't tell my mom what was happening, and the first answer is simple…I didn't want to get in trouble. I broke too many family rules by taking stuff I wasn't supposed to, so I felt I was in too deep. I had to handle this the best way I could without my ass becoming collateral damage by my mom if you know what I mean.

One day, I was told that Chester wanted me to run to the store for him, I went downstairs, and he opened the door butt-assed naked! I had never seen an adult male before in the nude at all. I think I saw the back of my dad's butt one time when he was in the shower when I was like three or four when we lived on the base, but outside of that never. He tried to get me to come into the house, but I told him my mom was timing me because she wanted me to hurry up and come back with the item she needed to cook. Crisis averted.

TRANSFORMED

A few days after that, I guess he felt like it was time to really make his move. I was headed downstairs to go outside, and he opened the door and told me to come in because he had something he wanted me to give to my mom. I felt my stomach drop. I remember that deep sinking feeling in the pit of my stomach like it was yesterday and I can still see this playing out in slow motion.

Reluctantly, I walked into his apartment, and he closed the door behind me and went toward the kitchen. At first, I started to feel relief, because it seemed like he was getting something to give to me. As I waited, I remember looking around and seeing he had a whole bunch of toys and children's games. This struck me as odd because Chester didn't have any kids and we never saw any family members visiting him, so I was wondering why he had all this stuff for kids. The uneasy feeling started to creep back in, and I began to move closer to the door. He comes back from the kitchen with his robe open and something in his hand. I do not remember what it was, but he stopped right in front of me and handed me whatever it was, so I said okay and put my hand on the doorknob.

He beat me to it and stopped me; at that point, I pleaded with him to let me out so I could go home. He asked me to stay a little longer and I told him no. That was when he reached out and squeezed my breast. I screamed loudly and pushed his hand away. I don't, at this point, recall what I screamed, but whatever I yelled spooked him, and he yoked me up by my arm, opened the door, threw me out, and told me never to talk to him again.

After that, he never looked my way, gave me any money, or even acknowledged my existence. A short time later, I saw that he began to pay attention to this other little girl who was probably around five years old. I wanted to say something, but I didn't have any proof of anything, and I didn't know what to say because if I felt like if I told on him, I would get in trouble because I had been taking all that money and stuff from him knowing for a fact my family always instilled in us children to never take anything from anybody.

I kept my mouth shut and one day as I was coming out of my apartment to head downstairs down, I saw him take that little girl into his apartment. Mind you, I'm only nine years old but I still remember the dread I felt about that and the guilt that I carried for a long time that I didn't say anything to save her from whatever may have happened in that apartment.

My mom, like so many other moms in that building, was a struggling single mom raising two children, who were both in private school. Struggle was a staple in our household, but she was doing the best she could, having gone back to school to get her GED, going to college for journalism (yup, writing, I got that from my Momma) until she had to drop out, but went to secretarial school to acquire a skill and landed a job at NJ Transit all on her own. It was freaking rough, but she did it, and we were only on assistance for a short while until she accomplished those things. Were there family members who could have helped my mom along the way to make it easier for us? Yes. Did they? Nope. Not sure of their reasons, but it made my mom work harder for us and I learned how to survive from her. No, my mom wasn't perfect and made a lot of mistakes, but she was persistent, very present, independent, and never gave up. So very proud of you, Lady!

I say all that to say that sometimes, things got tight and like so many of the tenants, she might fall a little behind on some bills, but she was trying to make ends meet like everybody else. She would need an extension on the rent and Chester would always talk to the superintendent and we would get it. But the tide turned suddenly and not too long after that situation happened with Chester, we were evicted from our apartment, and I overheard my mom saying that normally they would give her an extension to catch up on the rent but this time they were adamant about us leaving.

I know that came from Chester who had the owner and superintendent's ear. The guilt that I felt knowing that because I did not comply with what this man wanted from me, I was the reason why my family was being thrown out of this apartment. That guilt and feeling of letting my family down and the regret of maybe I should have let him do whatever he was going to do, which was hazy to me because I knew about sex from "the talk" but that was the extent of my experience. Or better yet not taking the money and gifts from him in the first place. The fact is, I should have known better and not put us in that position, stayed with me for such a long time.

Again, this is the mind of a nine-year-old who should not even have to think about these things because there should be no grown-ass man trying to sleep with an adolescent child.

I kept my mouth shut and didn't tell my mom or anybody in my family after we moved, not because I felt like they wouldn't believe me but because of the fear that they would believe me, and they would probably kill him. I would have been responsible for a family member going to jail.

For some reason, I've always carried this weight on my shoulders of being responsible for my family, making the best decision that I possibly could to help my family, and making sure that everybody was good even to my own detriment. I wouldn't find out why that was until later in my spiritual quest.

For a while, my brother and I had to move in with my grandmother in Irvington and I do recall an incident involving this man in her building not long after we arrived. I was getting on the elevator to go to my grandmother's apartment, and he got on the elevator with me and tried to solicit me to come to his apartment.

He told me the apartment that he was staying in, and I told him repeatedly that I was just a little girl, to which he replied, "But you don't look like a little girl." Sir, what does that even mean!?!?!

I was so afraid of what he was going to do or if he was going to try to snatch me and pull me into his apartment, I pressed myself up against the back of that elevator until he got off and the elevator doors closed.

I went one floor up to my grandmother's apartment, and it just so happened that one of my uncles and one of my big cousins was visiting her that day. My grandmother must have seen the look on my face because she immediately asked what was wrong.

I could barely get the words out and as I suspected, my uncle and my cousin grabbed me up, asked me where he lived, and proceeded to march me down to his apartment.

They started banging and trying to kick the door in, yelling for that man to come out! Of course, he was smart and didn't, because they stood over six feet and were built like gladiators. I'm not sure how long we were out there but they sent a clear message that if he ever came near me again, they were coming back to kill him.

I never saw that man again, ever! This was the exact reason why I didn't tell them about Chester, but in hindsight, I totally wish I had. Thirty years later, I finally told my mom what happened regarding

TRANSFORMED

Chester and the guilt I carried to which she was adamant that it was her responsibility with regards to what happened with the eviction, not mine of course. I was able to release that burden finally and it was such a healing moment for us both.

For the life of me, I could not figure out why these things were happening. Was it because of the way that I looked? Was I looking too grown up? Was I acting too "fast"? Which of course, wasn't the case because I was one of those kids with the body of an adult but the mind of a child for real.

It was at this point I really began to overeat as a defense mechanism, but I also began to weaponize food as a form of revenge if my family brought it up that I was too fat or getting too big, which by that time, I was about 5 '4 and about 130 pounds. But a very dangerous pattern was beginning to form. If they did or said something I didn't like, I would eat in retaliation. Since I would be the one to clean the kitchen after dinner, I would steal extra spoons of food while putting it away. Then I started stealing candy and junk food from the corner store or bodega, hiding it by cutting the lining of the pockets in my coat where the contraband would fall in the lining, so when they patted my pockets, they were empty. I hid food in my dresser, bookbag, and closet, or I would binge eat the junk food on the walk back home. That little budding flame of anger and resentment with my home life was fanning into a full blaze by now.

Religious Tea

My school life at St. Lucy's Elementary from first grade to 8th grade was great! I grew up with the same set of kids in a small private Catholic school, so I didn't have to experience a lot of the ridicule and bullying I might have experienced in public school because nuns don't play that plus a lot of the kids knew what happened to me from when I was little kid. I grew up with these friends from the age of five, so they knew my story and I was safe in that environment. Also, I was a very good Catholic student, because just like at home, I believed everything the nuns were teaching us about God and religion verbatim. I always received A's in religion, I was baptized by the Monsignor at St. Lucy's church when I was a baby and spent my wonderful years at the school. At school, like home, I saw the nuns as infallible beings, who knew all, saw all, and were the focal point of my world. The priests were these larger-than-life but very removed father figures that you both revered and feared.

Fun Fact: when I graduated, we had a school assembly and I performed the speech, "Can We Wave the Flag Too Much?" which won me a gold medal in that year's oratory competition. The Monsignor gave me a compliment and advised him to see great things in my future. I was elated!!!!

I didn't realize until later that this is how I viewed the men in my family and God. These beings were larger than life, feared, revered, and just right out of reach. The only time they were there was to hand out judgment, good or bad, whether it was a scolding or money. You vied for their attention, but they made little time for you…more of big picture figures whereas the women and nuns were day-to-day boots on the ground brigade. So, God the Father, to me seemed the same way, same as his son…there but not there. I gravitated more toward Mother Mary and looked forward to her celebration. I always had trepidations with God, he seemed so angry and wrathful to me, and the more I learned, the more removed from me he became. He just didn't make me feel safe, quite the opposite. Because I grew up as a Catholic, it is frowned on to go anywhere near any occult stuff, like astrology, tarot, magic, etc. But honestly, I was also always drawn to ghost stories, soothsayers, and all that jazz. I used to love sitting down and listening to stories Mamma told me about seeing spirits or her mother (whom we called actually called Mother), telling stories of the different roots she witnessed as a child placed on folks that wronged someone down south, or the haints, and other "spooky" real life accounts of things that folks whispered about. These stories fascinated me to no end. Again, everything we come across is designed with your true path in mind and this little side fixation was no different.

Plus, do you recall how my prayers sounded like mantras? Well, by this time I had created another mantra that formed into a rule, I didn't even know I manifested it until many years later. While watching my mom struggle as much as she did, I vowed I would not have children until I made a million dollars…not over time either but at one time. And boy it worked…I do not have kids to this day! All these spiritual paths were running parallel at the same time.

Here Comes High School

I didn't experience my first real bullying until I graduated from St. Lucy, entering my freshman year at Our Lady of Good Counsel when I was twelve. While many of the St. Lucy students also went on to O.L.G.C., thus knowing quite a few upperclassmen, there were so many people I didn't know who didn't know my origin story. A couple of boys (quite unattractive, I may add…like they were the melanite version of Laurel and Hardy) were making disparaging remarks about me, both about my weight and my teeth, and for the first time I didn't like coming to school, not because of the schoolwork but the people.

I had never had to deal with that in a classroom setting before and I was shaken. Being a freshman and soon-to-be teenager was stressful enough but bullying added insult to injury. Little did I know that sometimes you can get help from the most random people. This is when you know it's Divine Intervention.

I remember that there was this fellow freshman girl who was kind of mean sometimes, and she was standoffish with me most of the time. She found out that I was being bullied and why from one of

TRANSFORMED

our mutual friends that she did like. One day, my friend heard them talking about me and went off right in the middle of the homeroom period. She told them they didn't know me or what I went through and had no right to make fun of what they didn't understand. First of all, let me tell you, my best friend, whom I had known since we were first graders was the happiest person I think I had ever met. She never said an unkind word to me or anyone, nor had I ever seen her get mad like that until that day! The other girl asked my bestie what happened to me and then she went off and told them to apologize, which they did. Of course, the entire incident went around the school and got back to a few upperclassmen I knew, who made it a point to "drop by " one of my classes with their popular crew, and from that point on, no one bullied me again. It was a great feeling to have so many folks have my back, but unfortunately, it was a precursor of what was to come.

The Birth of the Clap Back

I can still say that I was getting a form of bullying from my family in reference to my weight. I had nicknames like "hippie dip", and "tank". I had a family member come to my grandfather's house one day and we were also visiting him at that time. This uncle decides to greet me with "Hey, fatty" and before I could stop myself, I responded, "Hey, Blackie!" which I knew would sting because he was dark-skinned. You know when the needle on the record scratches, that is what that moment felt like! Time stood still for what seemed like an eternity. I was frozen, my brother Haneef stood stock still looking at me, at first in shock, then awe. Suddenly, the grown-ups in the room found their voices and erupted in outrage, calling for my head on a platter and my ass whooped immediately! My mom, God bless her, stood her ground in my defense, stating what grown person would greet a child like that and think it's okay? For the first time, I stood up for myself and the clap back in me was born!

After that, I began to get really mean, and for a long time, I was known for being not so nice and this was a shock coming from the "very nice, good little girl."

Around this time, I began to pick up some real weight from all the hiding and stealing food. I went from 5'5 and 130 to 140 to 150 and then slid to 160 by the time I was in my sophomore year.

I also had my first heartbreak at that time because I liked a very popular boy who of course did not like me because I was bigger. I remember feeling unattractive at this time of my life, weight gain, my teeth, and let's add acne in for good measure, because it's not like I need anything else to go wrong!

The only thing I had was my intelligence. That was the thing that I fell back on was the fact that I was smart and creative. That's what they couldn't take away from me. I would carry that with me to this day. I don't care what you say about me. I don't care if you don't like the way I look, how I speak, or carry myself, it doesn't matter. I know for a fact I'm intelligent, creative, and talented in so many areas. There is a difference between a belief system and something that you know, because if you know you know, you can't be swayed, but belief systems can change. If you know something in your core, they can never take that away from you. Remember that.

Towards the middle of my sophomore year, my mom took a fateful trip down south to Georgia and came back with this bright ass idea to relocate there.

Moving to Georgia??? My junior year???

Talk about the devastation because I had my entire life planned out of course. Things were kind of looking up. I found out that a couple of boys that I was a little bit interested in kind of liked me, so that was going to be interesting come next year when I can date! Plus, I was already popular in school and was going to be an upperclassman! I was going to either stay at this school or my mom was considering letting me try out for Arts High because I wanted to sing and act. Afterward, if I wasn't already discovered, I would attend Montclair State with my besties, and probably marry one of these boys from high school if I didn't marry Prince. Again, I had my entire life planned out. I am a Capricorn, it's what we do.

TRANSFORMED

So, for my mother to come in and make the announcement that we were not moving across town, not even to New York, which we visited every other weekend, would have been amazing. I love New York. We used to go there just to hang out at Washington Square Park or walk up and down 42nd Street. It was nothing to go to New York on the weekend.

Aaahhh the memories....

But noooo, she's moving us to the South where we knew not a soul. The closest relatives we had were very distant and they lived in Dublin, wherever the hell that was.

She announced we were moving to the Atlanta metro area, or more specifically, a place called Lithonia, where I would attend Public School! And another thing...My grandmother wasn't coming. WTF!?!?!?! Are you kidding me? Now my mom is my rock, but my grandmother is my mom's rock...how in the hell is the rock's rock not coming???

This couldn't have gotten any worse than if she said the devil was going to be our new roommate. I was so upset and depressed but there was nothing I could do about it. I do remember when we were getting closer to moving, my brother asked if they had McDonald's there. He asked some of the craziest questions about bathrooms inside of the house and things like that, but McDonald's was the last straw. Me being the big sister and going through I guess what the kids would have called emo at that time or really just being an asshole teenager, I remember telling him, "I don't know if they have McDonald's down there, they probably do. But you know what else they really do have… the Atlanta child murderers and from what I understand, they kill little boys like you."

Now, that was some horrible shit to say to your kid brother who was by that time probably about nine, but again, of course, you know I'm a teenager, I'm 15 years old, my entire life is being taken away from me, my very best friends and my whole future (you see where the drama comes in) so I was being a dick, I'll admit that.

On the last day, we were in our apartment, a couple came up from downstairs and said they were ministers and wanted to know if they could pray for us. My mom said yes, and they proceeded to first pray and then instructed us to "get saved" by giving our lives over to Christ. I had seen this before in my dad's family church as well as my grandfather's, but no one ever asked if we wanted to do this…we are Catholics.

But we went through the ritual and gave over our life to someone that I supposedly already had a relationship with but hey, what do I know?

After that, we piled in the U-Haul and took a pit stop to say goodbye to our dad. I remember him stating that we could stay with him if we wanted to, and my mom said it was our choice. But as much as I hated the idea of moving down south, my mom was my world, so I hauled my ass back in the U-Haul and we headed for ATL.

CHAPTER 3

Trials And Tribulations

Before I Begin

This might be the hardest chapter I will write. This part of my life holds so much pain and heartache that the thought of reliving it on paper had me procrastinate writing this book four years later than I had anticipated. There will be many people in my life who will read this and think, "But she seemed happy, she was always cracking jokes." or "But we had such a good time!" Yeah, that's the thing, people tend to look at your life from their lens, not necessarily through yours. Not because they don't want to, well maybe some people are too self-absorbed to really want to see the people around them, but some just don't have the capacity or point of reference to be able to understand or discern what is going on in someone's life.

In the following pages, I'm going to pull in the lowest moments that contributed to my weight gain. I don't think I can emotionally cope with describing in detail every single emotional upheaval in these

27 years. This huge chunk of my life is full of self-loathing, depression, anxiety, and just not fitting in. I was very adept at assimilating fitting in, but I have always felt like I didn't quite belong.

Even now, as I sit here, under the strict rule I made for myself, which is that I cannot leave from my office for the day until this chapter is complete, I am still distracting myself with my fur baby, Sebastian, the internet, fixing the blinds and anything else I can think of to avoid the inevitable.

Shit.

No more running.

Just breathe.

Welcome to Atlanta

I was putting on weight little by little, but it was noticeable by the time we moved to Georgia going into my junior year. I was 5'5 which is the height I am now at about 170-175 pounds, so I was officially overweight at that point. I didn't hear it from my friends in Jersey as I was one of the cool kids and had lots of friends but that was not the case when we relocated to Georgia. That's when I officially became "big."

TRANSFORMED

Now, the term for being overweight has changed over the course of my life, depending on the scale. For Melanite people, we don't use the term fat unless we are talking about a really sloppy person. Black folks will use the terms "big," "plus-sized," "big boned," "biggum," "meaty," "fluffy," "thick," "juicy "or the latest "big-back!" We'll use every term in the book before we say fat, so as to not hurt someone's feelings unless you want to clap at them, and then suddenly, they're a fat ass, or some other variation that includes the word fat. For the most part, you are just big and that is the adjective used to describe me throughout my adult life. I'm a big girl. Not fat, overweight, or obese, which is where I was headed, but just big. I remember people saying, "Oh no, you're not fat, you are just big," as if there is a difference. I guess in their mind, if your personality is great, you are well put together, you don't smell, you're dressed nicely and an overall nice person, you're just a big girl, and that's cool. Well, not that cool.

At the time I was in high school, there was no such thing as "body positivity." Folks weren't going around defending the big girls, and thick girls were not in style just yet. Video Vixen bodies hadn't even become a thing, so petite girls ruled the school. There weren't a whole lot of folks checking for the big girls around that time. Now, I am not saying that was the case for every big girl and guy out there, I'm saying what I saw and experienced in my own world around me.

I was fifteen, entering the eleventh grade at Lithonia High School, and up until that point, I wasn't allowed to date or go out with boys unless it was in a group setting. Yes, I come from that era with that type of mom! By the time I was allowed to date, I was in Georgia, and my status went from popular to pariah, just like that. I was the new kid, from the north, when there weren't many transplants in the south like there are now. They made fun of my size, my clothes, and even my accent, so I didn't have many friends. On one of my first few days in the lunchroom, someone exclaimed, "Oh, you a Yankee!" True story.

I made one friend, Tina in my neighborhood, who I was lucky enough to have moved in next door to her family and she became one of my best friends to this day. She happened to be very popular, which allowed me to hang out with some of the popular kids adjacent. The problem was, she was a freshman, and that two-year separation was like 10 dog years in high school! For a better part of my junior year, kids thought I was a smart freshman who took junior classes!

Coming from a private school, I was very advanced, so my junior and senior years contained a lot of electives. If I had my way, I would have doubled up on the required classes and graduated at sixteen, but no one else agreed, so my roster was filled with classes I just didn't need but one of which I loved was chorus. Here is where I met another close friend who was super popular but for a very specific reason.

This girl, a sub-freshman whom we will call Vixen, was infamous in several school districts before social media and cell phones…that's saying something! Even though she had a "reputation" we hit it off and became best friends. She was also instrumental in introducing me to her friend, Ruby, as we were the two friends she chose to have at her sweet sixteen sleepover and although Vixen and I are no longer friends, Ruby and I remained close to this day.

Lithonia High for me was not a great time in my life. To fit in, I joined the track team with Tina, but I hated it. I was a big girl, so they put me on disc and shot put…it was horrible, and I was horrible at it. What kept me going, even though at the end of the season I didn't even get a letter, was my coach. My track coach was amazing, took zero-ish, and had a soft spot for me a little. I think she saw my struggles and allowed that part of school to be a safe space.

When word got around about my little handicap with my teeth, the lunchroom became a hell loop where there were entire tables making fun of me. At one point, Vixen and I, whose lunch period and study hall were built in with the chorus, started to sneak into the lunchroom right as the bell rang and took our lunch downstairs to the chorus room. A haven for us both as she was also not well-liked by the girls in school. This went on during my first year, but by the second year, things died down and the place became bearable.

Senior year was not going to turn out like I envisioned when I was still in Jersey, but it was okay. I made it a point to sit with the Seniors in the cafeteria before classes (I picked the most non-threatening table I could find.) And before you know it, I was a part of the group. I also started to make friends in certain classes when they realized I was in fact a senior, and I was smart (duh, all my classes were advanced) and was personable and funny when you get to know me.

Having cool teachers also made it a little better like my computer teacher, who was super cool, and my English teacher who encouraged me to go to U.C.L.A. and stated I was good enough to be a writer. And there was my chemistry teacher in my junior year and during her class, some of the guys used to make fun of me and one day I just walked out.

I went to the girls' lavatory and stood there thinking, hoping, wishing they would just leave me alone. When I got back, fully expecting her to send me to the principal's office but she just said to sit down and continue teaching, but they never did it again. A classmate told me later that she threatened to fail anyone who said anything negative to me for the rest of the school year. She was one of those who carried out a threat, so they knew she meant it.

TRANSFORMED

Thank God for small miracles and miracle workers.

I also joined the drama club in my senior year, dropping track (whew!). My heart and soul were very much into pursuing a singing and acting career in Hollywood while attending UCLA for writing. There was drama at home, and I was very much missing my friends and family in Jersey, so chorus and drama were pretty much the bright spots in my life. I never dated in high school at all and didn't attend either prom, which was a far cry from me attending all the dances and functions we had at St. Lucy and OLGC. I was known as the sidekick to Tina, like when you date a woman with kids, and you know the kids are a package deal. Then, I was the gatekeeper or the "brain" to Vixen because you had to get through me to get to her. One guy said we were known amongst the dudes as the Body and the Brain. I'm not sure which one of us was more offended.

My relationship with Ruby was so different from Vixen. We were both a little different and knew it! We loved the same music and fashion, and even though we didn't realize it at the time, we started the art of manifestation early. I recall us driving around aimlessly at night talking about the future and then ending up at Waffle House drinking coffee, we made up scenarios of our lives in the future and spoke as if it was happening at the moment. Life has a funny way of dropping little nudges to help you on your intended path.

TRANSFORMED

Finally, I graduated and went on to attend GA State University, as my mom could no way afford to send me to California. I chose Communications, with a concentration in PR because it had the least amount of math requirements. I had zero attachment to what I was going to school for. I just knew my family wanted me to go to college. No one guided me on what I should be or do, the consensus was to go and so I went.

I still lived at home because at that time there wasn't a campus, but I made friends, hung out with some folks in the Divine Nine and was finally learning about Black Greeks and was even going to pledge in my sophomore year with the support of a Soror!

Things were looking up.

Then I had an accident at my job which caused me to leave school and I didn't go back for years.

Right before I was hitting my twenties, something devastating happened. I was raped at gunpoint by my drunk boyfriend, and I will not mention his name but if you want to come forward and claim what you did so that everyone knows you're a rapist, please feel free. I was beaten, plugs of my hair pulled out and I always had a habit of wearing long acrylic nails and he bent some of them off which made my nails start bleeding. He was going to do it in front of my house, but my family was in there and there was not going to be anyone hurt by this man but me, so I convinced him to drive to a remote area to do what he wanted. After it was done, he drove me back and dropped me off with a feeble apology. I got out of the car, and he drove off. I walked into the house and went upstairs, took off my clothes, buried them in the bottom of the hamper, and took a shower.

I trusted and loved this person and thought this person loved me but reflecting on our entire relationship now, I can see that this was a classic case of domestic abuse. First, was the emotional and verbal abuse as well as attempted isolation from your loved ones. You don't see it right away because it happens so gradually, so by the time you see there is a problem, your self-esteem takes a hit, and you feel like you don't deserve better. He accused me of cheating and always had issues with me hanging out with friends and even my family. There wasn't anything I did that was right, except spend my hard-earned money on him as he couldn't keep a job.

Did I report it? No. First, I was too shocked and confused by what happened that I was not even sure if it was really rape since I had a sexual relationship with this person. It took Ruby, who was away at college at the time, to convince me. When I told her what happened and that it wasn't really rape that… "Yes, it was!" She insisted, trying to convince me. Still, I didn't want to come forward because we all see what happens to rape victims who report their assault…a public rape all over again.

I shut it down and just suppressed it. Compartmentalized it. I moved on, but I didn't really move forward. There was a certain arrested development that happened at that point, it was like a part of me was frozen in that moment and never got a chance to move forward because I never allowed myself to deal with what had happened from a therapeutic standpoint.

So, I kept it moving, but it affected how I approached dating or lack thereof after that. I think I had maybe one brief relationship after what happened, and then I went for a stretch of a few years without dating. I would be attracted to men, but I think at that point, I started to build a barrier so men wouldn't get that close to me. I began to think maybe I didn't deserve or wasn't worthy of love and this was manifesting in physical weight.

That first rapid weight gain was around 22 years of age when I went from around 190 to about 230. That's when it was proposed to me that I might have PCOS, which is polycystic ovarian syndrome. With this disease comes rapid weight gain and the inability to lose it, facial hair, and hair loss (which I didn't experience, thank God) I had a whole head of thick hair, and it makes it very difficult to conceive (another win as having a baby with my previous boyfriend would have been catastrophic), so I don't really know if I even had PCOS, that was just a theory that one of my gynecologists had that might be the reason behind my rapid weight gain.

TRANSFORMED

The next few years went by with me having a host of odd jobs until I landed in this one collection call center and met a few people who would change my life. The first was Adriane, hailing from Brooklyn and a recent graduate of Clark Atlanta, whom I took a liking to instantly. Turns out over the years she would become the big sister I always wanted. I also met a trio of friends from Chicago and one of them, I call Mr. Chicago, introduced me to meditation, and other spiritual practices like Egyptology and challenged me for the first time to start figuring out who I was and what I really wanted.

At that time, I was practicing Christianity, Charismatic or Pentecostal…I think…and traveling with an Evangelist on weekends as a driver (which was hella fun, a lot of tea of that world was overheard while being an assistant) then when she moved her church to South Carolina, I joined another church and became full Gospel Baptist until they slighted my friend's boyfriend after he asked for financial assistance. So, Mr. Chicago was presenting something so taboo but, at the same time, dare I say, exciting? But I didn't have the guts then to go all the way down the rabbit hole with him. However, I did manage to shake him with tales of my prophetic dreams. Especially when I had one while knowing him and then later it came to fruition.

Oh wait, did I fail to mention that?

My bad, my interest in the spirit realm was not just by happenstance, no it came from within. I recall as a child I was fixated on Saturn, my absolute favorite planet, not knowing that it is Saturn that rules the sign of Capricorn, which I am. Also, I have had a series of dreams where I am speaking to people in my family who were long gone before I was born. I have had premonitions of things about to take place. I have even had prophetic dreams and told people about them, and they came to pass. It's funny how natural gifts like the gift of sight unless operating under the church umbrella, are deemed demonic, but inside the church setting is the divine gift of prophecy. I've never understood that.

Okay, now you are caught up FRFR.

So, I will credit Mr. Chicago for putting me on the path or the yellow brick road, but it would be a few more years before I really threw caution to the wind and embarked on that journey. However, he did encourage me to get back on the path of entertainment, not in front of the camera but behind it. So, off I went to attend the Art Institute of Atlanta.

I was in my late twenties at this time and worked a myriad of odd jobs, including being an Uber before there was such a thing. I couch-surfed for a while before my mom, who had since moved back to Jersey to care for my grandfather, returned and I was able to live with her. Up until that time, I hadn't dated and now that I was a starving student, my weight held steady at around 230 pounds. School was amazing and it turned out that I was a phenomenal producer. Whenever there was a group project, I was always the first to be looped in as the producer, and I loved it! I met a whole new set of folks from all walks of life and ages who were artistic, inquisitive, driven, and freaking crazy! My kinda folks! Aside from being broke most of the time, still single, and credit shot to hell, I felt hope. Things were looking up and I felt like I was finally back on track.

Ummm….

Trigger Alert.

This next part may be difficult for some of you to read so I want to forewarn you.

If I thought that last assault was bad, it had nothing on what I was going to experience and once again, at the hands of someone that I was involved with. This, my friends, was what you call an abusive relationship, and my self-esteem and self-worth were so low that I didn't walk away after the first incident happened.

The first attack happened in my friend, Tina's car, which she had allowed me to borrow to go visit him. I am not sure what triggered him. I really don't know, but it was like one minute he was fine and then the next he flipped. I was raped vaginally, sodomized, and I was forced to perform oral sex, and held physically hostage for hours. I'm not talking about not letting me out of the bed or the house, no, he laid on top of me in a car for all that long time, holding me down while I struggled, cried, begged, and screamed for him to let me up. He mocked me the entire time like it was a game.

Finally, as the sun was coming up, he let me up and got out of the car. I pulled on my clothes and left without saying a word. I was a total blank all the way back to Tina's house, and when I recounted the story because she and her boyfriend at the time were pissed that I was so late bringing back the car, I felt like they didn't believe me. Hell, I didn't believe me. Then I tried to rationalize that maybe it wasn't that bad, but the blood in me from being sodomized was proof it was just that bad.

I didn't contact him for a while, didn't call, visit, and wouldn't take his calls. One day, Tina and I went to see a mutual friend whom he's related to, and he was there. I didn't get out of the car, but he came over and quietly apologized and told me he missed me. I was okay. Then he asked if would come back to visit him. I told him I would think about it. Later, I decided to give him another chance. Please don't ask me why, I can't even tell you that. All I can think is that how I felt and viewed myself was so low that I believed I couldn't get any better and maybe he was truly sorry.

That was the night that changed my life. As soon as I got there, I thought we might talk through what happened, but he became very verbally abusive and threatening. He forced me to have vaginal and oral sex. It was violent, like the kind of violence that makes you feel like you are not going to make it. His family was coming home soon so we went outside, mind you it was winter, and I had on a brand-new sweater with a fur collar. He had me outside for what seemed like an eternity, I asked to use the restroom and he forced me to relieve myself outside like an animal. I feared this time I might not make it. Throughout that night, I held an image of my bed in my bedroom in my head, and I kept thinking, I just want to get back there... that's safe. Remember a game we used to play as kids and we picked a place that was home base where you were safe, that was called base. My bed...that was base. I was like, "If I could just get back there, get back there, get back there." I kept that visual in my head the entire time.

At one point, he told me to get down on my knees and perform oral sex, and I told him no, I wanted to go home. He slapped me so hard and so fast; that I was confused about whether I imagined it. While I was reeling from that, he proceeded to tell me again to perform oral sex on him and he pushed me down on my knees. This time, something in my head clicked as I was on my knees staring at his crotch. I thought, "If I'm going to die tonight, (because I believed that I was), I am going to die on my feet fighting."

I jumped up, screamed "NO!" (Another time I literally found my voice), and we started fighting. His people came outside and pulled him off me, and I literally was pulled out of my sweater. I hauled ass for my car, leaving a fistful of my hair in his hands. As I was running, somebody was calling after me, and I thought it was the devil because that's what he became to me at that moment.

I got to my car and realized it was my friend's girlfriend holding my brand-new sweater. I swear, I loved it so much, a brown sweater tied at the waist with a faux fur collar. She tried to get me to calm down before I got behind the wheel but all I wanted to do was get the hell away from there before he was able to follow me. I threw the sweater on, got in the car, and peeled off. When I arrived home, I took the sweater off along with the rest of my clothes and once again buried it in the bottom of the hamper and took a shower.

I finally got to home base, my bed; my head was blazing because of the beating and the handful of hair I lost. I tried to do the same thing I did the last time, but this time I couldn't suppress it. I don't even have the words to describe how much physical pain I felt, how much mental pain I felt. I couldn't compartmentalize this one this time and I was almost thrown out of school because I had so many missed days.

I shut down mentally, emotionally, and sexually for years after that. I saw him at two different social gatherings after that, both of which

TRANSFORMED

I wasn't aware nor advised he would be there, and it literally took me out when I saw him. I never traveled to that side of town. Not long after that, Tina and I had a falling out over a project we were working on together because of people in her ear turning her against me. I wound up turning my back on the entire crew I was hanging with, which included Adriane (trust me, I still hear about this from her to this very day). I think I removed myself from not only everyone who knew us but also that entire period because I just wanted out.

At this point, I was instilled with pure unadulterated fear. This time the fear permeated my entire being like a cancer spreading to every inch of my life. I developed fear and distrust of anyone new in my life, especially men and If I didn't already know you, I did not feel safe around you. Growing up with siblings and various family members living with me at one time or another, I used to relish being home alone and loved living alone but that was taken from me. I had moved into my own townhome not soon after graduating and landing a job as an editor for a show that aired worldwide. I think I was only there for about 20 days and had to break the lease because I could not sleep, and my health was deteriorating.

At the time, I thought it was just living alone, but it was also being in the house alone that frightened me. When I moved in with someone, if they spent the night out or weren't in the house at night, I literally could not sleep. I get that way sometimes, to this day.

Fear is a crippling thing; it really is the mind-killer, and it killed a lot of who and what I was. I didn't look at the world the same, I always checked for exits, I feared the worst in any situation, and it limited where I went and who I went with. Mind you, I didn't report that rape either because not only did I feel like no one would believe me, but I was also so very terrified of this person, and I never wanted to see him again.

After this, I really began to use food as a crutch. I started using food as a substitute for the love life I didn't have, the friends that I lost, and more importantly, the protection that I needed.

It took over a year to reconnect with Tina and Adriane, and by that time, we were all in different places and Tina had fully separated herself from the individuals that would put me in the path of my assailant, so I didn't have to worry about that. We had a heart-to-heart talk about what happened that night and she told me the family had a prayer circle that night against me, the perceived evil that was trying to destroy the family. I knew right then and there that there would never be any kind of remorse or regret on his part regarding what he did to me or how that affected the rest of my life.

Then, in 2004, I lost my job as an editor, the same year I found out my dad had terminal cancer. We had been estranged since 1998 after a phone call I made to him and the operator told him it was a collect call from his daughter in Atlanta, to which he replied, "I don't have a daughter in Atlanta." I could hear that he was drunk, but that just hit me too deeply, and I never called him again. I even had a dream that I was in a hospital room and the doctor came in and told me to call the family because it was time. I told Tina about the dream, and she said that maybe I should reach out to him. I dismissed it as my psyche telling me that my relationship with him was dead and I should just move on.

The next time I saw him was in 2003 when I went back to New Jersey for my grandfather's funeral, and he was there. He tried in his way to make amends by saying he would love for me to call sometimes, and in that moment, I decided to be an asshole in response to how I felt all these years. I told him coldly that it goes both ways and pretty much ignored him the rest of the time he was there.

Fast forward a year later, to find out he was dying and had less than two years to live. I then reached out and made amends, I called him and was able to gather holistic herbs to help his cancer and sent it to him (which the family never gave him). My brother and I decided that we would drive to Jersey at least once a month to visit him. I thought to myself that I could finally get to know my dad and be that daddy's girl I always craved. The first trip was on July 4th weekend, when my brother started a new job, so I had to make the trip alone.

I arrived on the third and went to visit him, when I walked in, they asked him who I was and he said, "My baby girl." I will never forget that. I spent the day talking about what was going on with me, I showed him pictures of his grandkids whom he never met. I was so happy to be there with him. The next day, July 4th, I remember him sitting up and he looked at me and said, "I don't want to be sick anymore." Soon after, he took a sharp turn for the worse and we had to take him to the hospital. He stopped talking after that. I stayed in the hospital all day and night alone with him. I told him how much I loved him; how much Haneef loved him. On the morning of July 5th, the doctor came in and told me to call the family as it was a matter of time.

I called the family, and my grandma Ann as well as all his brothers and sisters came. By this time, he was breathing very shallowly, so we were just talking to him and making jokes. Suddenly, I looked, and he had slipped away. My dad was gone. I didn't get two years. I didn't even get ninety days. I was scheduled to fly that morning back to Atlanta, so I didn't even have time to mourn with the family as an uncle of mine drove me to Mamma's place to get my stuff and then to the airport. I recall sitting in Newark airport, crying. I got on the plane, and I just cried, I couldn't stop, the shock and devastation of it all just hit me. A nice black elderly couple was sitting next to me and took care of me the whole way back.

Words cannot describe how it feels to lose a parent. I also can't describe adequately how cheated I felt. Just when I was going to get the relationship I always wanted, no, needed…God just took my dad? The years wasted being angry and the one time I was an ass, played over and over in my head like an endless hell loop. In my years of despair, I couldn't understand why, I couldn't even look at his picture or speak about him without falling apart, and I for sure wasn't talking to God. I feared him and loathed him. God was not a comforter, God was not a healer, and God was not a savior. God was nothing to me.

The more you weigh, the harder you are to kidnap. Stay Safe - Eat Cake.

Clearly, folks had an issue with that meme whether you loved it or hated it, but I laughed about it because it was true for me. Over the next few years, I threw myself into church and was a part of the drama ministry, which fed my need for production in general, but not my soul. I was in it but not 'of it' as I never truly felt connected to what was going on in church or how everyone else was feeling. Don't get me wrong, I loved the people as I met some amazing, talented people during that time and had a lot of good times fellowshipping with them, but I never felt I belonged. On top of that, I began to get bigger and bigger. Dating was not a factor at all, even though I said I wanted to date, get married, and have a family but something was stopping me.

Subconsciously, I believe the bigger you are, the more intimidating you seem which means the less likely you are to be physically overpowered. Also, the bigger you are, the less attractive you'll seem, the less likely you will be assaulted.

So even though I may have said I wanted a relationship, even though people may have said I had such a pretty face, I personally blamed the fact that I'm not dating and I'm not appealing to the opposite sex, because I was big. They don't want a big girl. I took myself out of the equation, therefore I don't have to deal with men. I was safe.

That was my personal mantra. That was my reality, that was the rule that I created in my universe, and me creating that in my universe excused me from having to deal with the possibility of interacting with the opposite sex.

Then there were the wonderful people in my life who would say, "You see that big girl right there?" (That always cracks me up... people will find a person to use as an example), "She's twice as big as you (always twice…but they were just as big, LOL!) "And she has a man and he's a pretty good-looking dude!" And I would respond that I don't know what her situation was, but they don't want me because I am big.

This put me in the category of actively "verbally-only" seeking a relationship. So, what that means is, that I was actively verbalizing that I wanted a relationship and that I was seeking a relationship, but I could not find a relationship, I wasn't necessarily doing anything to seek out a relationship, nor was I being receptive to a relationship or to meeting anybody for said relationship. One must go out to meet people, and when you go out, you must have a certain sense of availability or inviting energy, frequency or vibe, and people will be attracted to what you're energetically putting out. So, even though you're saying, "I want to be in a relationship, and I want to get married, and have children." What you're projecting is a, "Get away from me muthafucka, run" energy, therefore the chances of you attracting what you say you want are slim to none.

So, that is my definition of actively verbally only seeking a relationship but doing absolutely nothing to facilitate that. Honestly, I wasn't even paying attention to men to see if anybody was looking at me or noticed me, and because I gave off that unapproachable vibe nobody ever did, and I became a self-fulfilling prophecy.

This behavior and lack of intimacy went on for years. I had a couple of very brief situations with emotionally unavailable men (I will get into that later as well) one of whom was definitely in it to sleep with what he called the biggest, sexiest person he ever met. The other was unavailable because he had a whole husband and was 'straight' on the low and fully gay in his real life. After that public humiliation, I went without any form of dating for the next eight years.

During this time, I was under a lot of stress, working a dead-end job making very little money. I had no romantic life, and my weight was steadily climbing the charts. My saving grace was that I did have family and friends, but when folks are involved in their own lives, they can't stand in for the other areas of your life that are lacking. Plus, as I said earlier, I was completely disconnected from God, Jesus, and the whole shebang. Anyone who tried to talk to me about God I was like, "Uh huh, okay." God did his thing, and I was doing mine.

Light a match…

I figured that was just how life was going to be, and the burden of life was getting heavier and heavier. The tunnel was long, lonely, and dark. I began to have panic attacks. I've suffered from migraine headaches for years, but now they come at least 3-4 times per month. My finances were suffering, my weight was skyrocketing as I had to be at least 380 by now and it was around 2014. I suffered from depression and anxiety. Did I seek professional help? Nope. Instead, I did what I've seen my family do, what I've seen folks in the ghetto do…light a match.

What I mean by that is that there are times when the tunnel you are in is so dark, and so long that you don't see a way out. There is no light as far as the eye can see, and you don't even know if there is even a light or is just another dark-assed tunnel. So, against your better judgment, you do things that are not in your best interest in the long run, but it gives you a small piece of fleeting happiness or light. Much like a lit match. Striking a match gives a burst of light but lasts only a moment. Not the best source of light, but sometimes, you need that just to make it to the next day, hell to the next moment.

This is when you know you have no money and no business spending a dime, but you say fuck it and buy an outfit, go out to eat, buy weed, alcohol, call that person you know ain't no good for you and sleep with them anyway. It's not the wisest decision, but at that moment, it's a brief respite from the darkness you are in. So, you make that call, spend that money, and deal with the fallout later. Sometimes you just need a win.

This was my life; a never-ending tunnel of shadow and it was getting darker by the day. Pockets of happy moments and lit matches weren't enough to balance the steady decline. Something had to give. I just didn't know what.

CHAPTER 4

2015: God Finally Talked Back

Just when you think it doesn't get any worse.

Like most folks, I do like to eat... don't get me wrong. I love some soul food, seafood, and Italian cuisine! The more sauce, the better! What's crazy is that I cannot remember the moment food switched from being a weapon (which I used as a kid) to a comforter. I didn't wake up one day and consciously used food as a comfort... I didn't say, "I ain't got a man, I'm going to eat." or "I hate my job, let me feed my failure."

I think relying on food as a point of comfort came on gradually. If I felt sad, I would eat to console myself. If I felt happy, I would eat to reward myself. It became a consolation prize, and it also became a grand prize. So, I didn't consciously make the decision to ritualize food, it was a natural, gradual thing that occurred. I don't think I knowingly recognized that pattern until 2015, but up until that point,

TRANSFORMED

I didn't realize food was becoming everything to me as far as a boyfriend, a lover, a confidante, or a companion.

By 2015, I didn't know If it was PCOS (which I still don't know if I truly had) the repeated assaults that happened to me, or by this time, the addiction to all the wrong foods that led to my rapid and steady weight gain. But BOOM! I did that. And like half of America, I would diet, or yo-yo diet for years to no avail. I can tell you some stories about the whole dieting experience.

I can, in fact, write a Bible book like the Book of Kings to tell my diet history. So may I present to you The First Book of Diets:

I begat the paid weight loss diet programs.

Then I begat the cabbage soup diet.

Then I begat the starvation diet.

Then I begat the grapefruit diet.

Then I begat the ice cream diet.

Then I begat the 3-day diet.

Then I begat the 4-day diet.

Then I begat carb only diet.

Then I begat meat only diet.

Then I begat the fruits and veggies only diet.

Then I begat the liquid diet.

Then I begat the blood type diet.

Then I begat the dieter's tea diet.

Then I begat the take these diet pills diet.

Then I begat the 2 shakes and meal diet.

Then I begat the famous beach diet.

Then I begat the make shit up as I went along starvation diet.

And all I was begetting was bigger.

Each time I began one of these amazing and fruitless endeavors I would drop maybe 20 pounds and those bitches would come back with a vengeance and bring friends. Seriously, during that yo-yo period, I steadily rose. I would drop down then rise higher, drop down again, and gain even more weight, and during all of that, like I said, people didn't really make my weight an issue, not in my face. It was few and far between that someone would make a disparaging remark about my weight. First, I didn't come across as a person that would take that shit, my mouth is lethal, so you don't want to battle wits with me. Second, my friends weren't going for that on any day of the week. There have been times when someone would make a comment that I didn't even hear, and my besties would be ready to fight!

Plus, I did what a lot of overweight people do which is berate myself openly about my weight before anyone else would get a chance to do it. This is a great defense mechanism because it takes the power away from anyone who would want to use your weight against you. Strike first so they have nothing to say. I was self-deprecating. I would talk shit about myself to take that power away from everyone else...

I love my family and friends. The more weight I put on, they would try to come to me and talk about how they were concerned with my health and worried about the mental and emotional toll it was taking on me. Their stance was that they had zero problems with my weight if I didn't have a problem with it, but they knew I wasn't happy in the skin I was in and that they were there to assist where they could.

I've had people try to help me and I have accepted that help and then lashed out severely, by either cussing them out or had such a nasty attitude to the point they wouldn't help me or bring it up again. At one point, no one would even talk about my weight anymore.

PSA: I didn't mean to be that mean or lash out, but it's a huge mental hell that an overweight person is in who does not want to be overweight, but it almost seems like they cannot help it. My apologies to all those who felt my wrath. My bad Boos.

Food is very addictive, and I was completely addicted to fast food, completely. During this time, I was eating fast food almost every single day. I was using food as a comforter, confidante, and crutch. And before you judge and think I wasn't addicted; it has been proven that they put a lot of shit in fast food to make you addicted so that you come back for more.

I recall many times I would pray and talk to myself in the car, "Do not stop anywhere, just go home and eat something else, just do not stop," and I found myself in a drive-thru crying because I didn't want to be there, but I couldn't help it.

These are real struggles that people go through, and folks don't understand food addiction, is just as powerful and detrimental as drug addiction. The difference between a drug addiction and a food addiction is that you have commercials on TV promoting all the wonderful fast-food and sit-down restaurants that I won't name because I don't want to get sued, but you don't have commercials on TV to promote drug use.

Imagine This Commercial:

Voice-over: "Nothing is better after a long day than a good pipe. This crack or crystal meth is freaking amazing, just look how the smoke rises from the pipe. This is gonna make you so high...doesn't it make your mouth water? "Mm mm good...

Right...

You will never see that. You can avoid a trap house, you don't have to go to places where they sell drugs or even alcohol, for that matter. But on every street corner, there are going to be fast food restaurants lights blazing, just calling for you. So, imagine if you had a drug addiction and, on every corner, there was this big blaring sign "drugs right here, 2 for 1," like double cheeseburgers or tacos all the time. Then you turn on the TV and there it is in your face, enticingly well-lit. What would you do? How hard or how much willpower do you think you would have?

You wouldn't.

"Just push yourself away from the table" speech is another thing that is so asinine. I absolutely hated it when people told me that because, newsflash, if I could, I would. Not only me, but every other overweight person would do just that but clearly, that's not happening. There is a much bigger issue going on and a little compassion and understanding goes a long way. Every day is a struggle, and some days are a win but most, not so much. I was so depressed and so despondent that I was just lost. It was a never-ending cycle. I felt like shit, so I ate. Then, the "food high" would hit and I felt briefly satisfied until I came down and I felt like shit again.

It's a life-sized hamster wheel that just keeps spinning.

Eating took on a certain intimacy for me. I would prefer to eat in solitaire. I used the times that I would eat as a ritual and people recognized that when I did eat in front of them. The way I lay out my food, how I prepared it. It was almost like foreplay. I did all this preparation before I ate it. The joke was that by the time I started eating my food, half the folks would be finished! My enjoyment starts with the preparation and presentation, and truth be told I still do that.

Presentation is everything to me!

Eating was a ritual for me, eating was comfort, eating was the closest thing that I had to making love outside of masturbation, it created the same sense of pleasure when I ate. It was just me, the food, and the television, and that was the three-some right there. And I was good, I was good with it. I don't think I recognized the pattern until the day I woke up fat in my head. I was like, I'm fat... and this isn't working anymore. What's happening? What are you doing? What are we gonna do? Because we can't do this anymore.

Now I've talked about what was going on outside, so let's talk about home life. At various times, it was kind of stressful at home for different reasons. Even when I live alone, loneliness can be stressful, and people do not realize that you are lonely because they aren't there to witness it.

Plus, I was very good at hiding my pain from the outside world. I put on the "Nia Show." A lot of people, I realized, who are overweight tend to over-compensate for the fact that they are hurting on the inside. They are living in their own private hell, which is why you see a lot of the funniest comedians use it as a defense mechanism whether they are overweight or not. You use it as a mask, you use it to hide inside... where it's not funny.

If people only knew how many times I made people laugh with my crazy humor, showing up at work, or at a function larger than life, but when I went home, I was in such a state of despair. I can't even think of an adequate word to describe the pain I felt inside, and food helped numb that for a time. Sometimes, I would try to push it out of my head and not think at all about it, and there were times when

I wanted to go to other means to numb the pain, like alcohol, and drugs, but in my head, I was like, "You can't have more than two vices."

I was big, so that's already one strike, if I overindulge in alcohol and do drugs, you're pretty much going to die quickly." I had too many overweight celebrities as role models to that fact. I might partake of alcohol every now and again, but I can't afford any more addictions. Trust me, I was tempted, because I was so depressed about a lot of things, about my physical body, about my career at the time, or lack thereof, and my love life but I was still trying to hold on...

Every day I felt like I was in a human coffin carrying around dead weight.

I always felt trapped because I'm always in my body, and I'm always cognizant of how big I am which dictates how I navigate in life. The world can be a dangerous and unforgiving place for obese people. If I was traveling out of town, I would either make sure I sat with friends on the plane or bought first-class tickets because of my size as I was too big at this point to sit in regular plane seats. I didn't want to spill over and invade somebody else's space, nor did I want them to make a scene by telling me I had to buy two tickets.

If I was going to restaurants, I would always ask for the name of the restaurant, not because I wanted to look at the menu but because I wanted to see the pictures of the inside of the establishment to see what kind of seating they provided. My biggest fears were the embarrassment of breaking a chair or not being able to fit in a booth. My friends understood the booth situation, so if they arrived at the restaurant first, they would automatically request a table to accommodate me.

This was everyday life for me, everything that I did, I had my weight in mind. If I was going to the mall, or if I was going walking with anybody, I would damn near try to kill myself to keep up. Feeling like my heart would explode in my chest because I just couldn't carry that much weight that fast. When you're overweight, the pressure on your ankles, the pressure on your knees, the pressure on your back, begins to take a toll if you are not meant to carry that load. Now, not only was I trapped physically, but I was also in pain, plus I would break out into a cold sweat when I was walking for a short distance. I couldn't really exercise, not because I didn't want to, but because the shit hurt so bad. Not to mention I couldn't catch my breath so it felt like I was suffocating, which would bring on a panic because I couldn't breathe which of course caused me to lose my breath even more.

I don't even think people understand what it feels like to not be able to catch your breath. I felt like I was about to see my maker in person at that moment and you're telling me to walk faster and press harder because I'm not working hard enough. People have no idea physically how taxing it is to move your body just to literally get out of bed and walk across the room when you get past a certain point in size for some people. It's excruciating. You can walk from your bed to the kitchen and you're breathing hard. You don't realize it, but your heart is pumping like nobody's business. It's trying its hardest.

I take my hat off for anybody overweight who finds the strength to do a workout when you are plus-sized because it's tough. I'm not saying everybody, because some big people have no problem going hard at the gym, I'm talking about those who are like I was, who struggled to get on a treadmill. Oh, and please don't try to talk to me, because I'm barely fucking breathing just walking on that thing. I was just going to nod or grunt at whatever the hell you are talking to me about because I can't afford any of that oxygen to go out and formulate any motherfucking words outside of "Help me" if I happen to be on the verge of collapse.

All I had in the reserves was "HELP ME!" If you heard that my ass was out of breath and she had nothing left to give, call 911, get the defibrillator ready, and do what you gotta do to save my life.

Picture this, Georgia 2015:

I remember sitting in my room one evening watching television when I felt the onset of a panic attack, but this one was different. Everything started spiraling and spinning, and I promise, I didn't realize it at first, but I started to claw at my chest, I looked down and thought to myself, "What the fuck are you doing?" What was I doing? I was trying to get out. I wanted out of this body, and it was so fucking heavy, and I don't know what happened at that moment, but I wanted out and I wanted to scream, and I felt the scream coming and I was thinking, If I scream, people in my house would think I was crazy. But I couldn't stop the shaking, or clawing at myself, and inside my head, I kept screaming, I wanna get out...

That was the moment when I woke up and said...YOU ARE FAT.

I wanted **OUT**!

But at that moment, I knew I couldn't get out. This is it. No matter how much I'm clawing at this body, I'm still in here, and in the next moment, I'm going to still be in it, and then the moment after that, and the next day, the next month, and on and on and on.

The thought, the feeling was too much. I didn't know how to handle this sudden epiphany, so I think I just zoned out and shut all my emotions off because I couldn't feel all of that at once. Whatever had happened, I couldn't handle the weight coming down on me, so I just shut it all down and got lost in whatever program was on television, and that was it. That began to happen more and more throughout the next few months. As a defense mechanism, each time it happened, I would shut my emotions down completely. If anyone would've walked in on me in those moments, I probably would have freaked them out staring ahead like a zombie in some sort of catatonic state. But that was the only way I had left to protect myself. To protect me mentally, because at that point, I was literally losing it.

A couple of years prior to 2015, I thought about having weight loss surgery. I went back and forth about it. The current insurance that I had didn't cover it, so I changed my election at the end of 2013 to one that would cover weight loss surgery, but I still hadn't actually made steps toward utilizing the benefit. I kept chickening out and putting it off because people were talking about how they knew somebody who had all these crazy complications or had a friend of a friend who died.

Now, here I was, the biggest I'd ever been, in a job that barely paid the bills and wasn't fulfilling. My creative career…wasn't. My creativity is tied to my emotional and mental state. If I am depressed or stressed, I cannot tap into that part that creates, so I was stuck in a vicious cycle. I hadn't written anything new; I hadn't done any of my individual projects, nor had I even tried to jump back into the industry, even in my old field of editing.

Don't even ask me about a relationship. I was at the age when most people are looking at their children getting ready to go off to college and I didn't even have a child yet, which I wanted, but according to modern medicine, my window had a sliver of light coming through but was about to seal shut.

Every aspect of my life was completely stagnant, and it was forcing me to face the fact that I'm at this stage in my life when most people are well-established in who they are, and what they want and are well on their way to achieving their goals. I was nowhere near any of that. To top it all off, I was teetering on some really big health problems. I was pre-everything. I didn't have anything yet, but everything was teetering, I was pre-diabetic, and I had pre-hypertension. Everything was on the verge of becoming something and one false move would bring the entire house down.

When it rains it pours.

Not that I needed anything else to go wrong in my life, but it seemed like the universe said, "Let's see what else we can pull from the bargain basement bin of bullshit." It seemed like right when I was hitting rock bottom, another bottom would appear, and I kept falling. I had an altercation with someone I considered one of my closest friends, and the realization of how they felt about me, my career choice, or my path was heartbreaking. What I did learn later is that sometimes the universe has a way of mirroring what you believe about yourself and mirror that through other people. I didn't believe in my own self-worth; my own talent, and destiny, and all these people did was verbalize my shadow self.

PSA: What is for you, is for you, no matter what anyone else thinks. The most important believer in your life and life path is YOU. Never allow anyone to write the script to your life…you are the Creator, Writer, and Director. PERIOD!

Plus, I had been struggling spiritually since my dad transitioned, and quite a bit of it also had a lot to do with the things that I had gone through, and I felt like God was not listening. He is literally turning his back when shit is happening to me. Not to mention, I had major trust issues with men, so with God being associated as a He, I didn't trust Him or feel safe.

Let's tally this up, shall we? I was huge, unhappy with my career, didn't have babies, didn't have a love life, and I was on the precipice of financial ruin (did I mention that?), and losing a bestie. All of that happened by April of 2015.

The first half of that year, more often than I care to mention, I contemplated suicide. I did not want to be here at all. I hurt mentally, physically, and spiritually. At this point in my life, with a few of my friends going through their own shit, it was the first time I felt truly alone and lonely.

My body was starting to break down from carrying that much weight. At this point, my belly was touching the steering wheel, and I was all the way back in the seat, pushing the gas and breaks with my toes. I no longer wanted to be social and hang out anymore. I was becoming more and more of a recluse and declining to go out because it was getting too hard.

On the one hand, I was thinking that I just can't continue to live like this anymore. This isn't living, it's just existing and it's not worth the trouble. On the other hand, I was also scared to die, and I know that sounds crazy for somebody who's contemplating suicide, but in the daytime, I wanted to take my life. Then the nights would come, and I would lay in my bed and think, "Oh God, what if I stop breathing and my family finds me dead in the morning?"

Honestly, I was more scared for my family. There was no way I wanted them to be burdened with my death. I have always had that sense of responsibility that I just don't want to be a burden to anybody. That was prevalent in my head like I wanted to die because I didn't want to live like this, but I didn't want to die because I had people relying on me. My grandmother lived with me and my brother at the time, and I had an obligation to be there for them. What would my death mean to them and my mom? I didn't want to put that on them, but at the same time, I just was not... well. I was tired, so very tired and broken.

Enter the straw that broke the camel's back...

I remember going out of town to a friend's birthday celebration in Mexico, and I was very excited to go because there were some pyramids I wanted to see. I love anything to do with ancient civilizations, so I was excited to see a pyramid up close and personal! We arrived there and everyone was having a great time with all sorts of excursions, but as the vacation moved along with all the physical activities, I was losing steam. When it was time to sign up for the pyramid excursion, I realized that it was a walking tour. I knew I couldn't do it. Aside from celebrating my friend's milestone birthday, the second main reason for even going was to see those pyramids and to realize that I traveled that far and was so close but because of my body, I could not walk that pyramid, was devastating.

To add insult to injury, on the last day of the trip, the ladies took a group photo like we always do to commemorate the occasion on the hotel steps, and I couldn't even go down the steps to be in the picture. So, I'm not even present in that memory which in my mind

TRANSFORMED

was a precursor to many more moments I may not be present for. I was pushed to the limit with that trip both physically and emotionally.

When I returned home, I remember one night crying out to God. I was like, "You know what God, even though I don't really talk to you like that... I don't wanna do this anymore. So, either kill me or help me, because I can't live the next 30 or 40 years like this if I even live that long. I'd rather you take me now and get it over with or help me change my life because I can't do it anymore."

Right after that, around September, one of my friends recommended a life coach she went to that helped her tremendously. At first, I wasn't receptive to it but one day something nudged me to give it a try, so I reached out to see if this would help me. She challenged me to talk about the past and try to find a resolution to help facilitate going forward with a better future. I remember getting to the end of the course, and I couldn't get past the last lesson. The last lesson consisted of looking back at my traumas and trying to make peace with what had happened to move forward, but the problem was I didn't have peace. I had one question and one question only…Why? I asked that question even though as Christians, we are not supposed to question God, but she was also a minister and therefore a representative, so I posed the question. Why? She was like, "What?" I said, "Why? Why did God allow these things to happen to me? I'm a good person, I need to know why, and I can't go forward until I know why." At that point, I realized what had been blocking me this entire time.

This is when I identified my arrested development. I needed to know why these things happened to me. I'm a good person, I'm a good daughter, a good sister, niece, friend, employee, and whatever other title or label you want to place on me regarding my roles in this life. I didn't deserve all that had happened to me in my life, I can understand peaks and valleys, but it seemed I spent most of my life in the valley, so I wanted to know why. She looked at me and replied, "Sometimes we don't get the why, and sometimes bad things happen to good people."

Bullshit.

I couldn't accept that answer. I remember crying right there in her dining room because I knew that was the nail in the coffin for me and God. I never finished the end of the course because I couldn't get past that shit. I couldn't get past so many others who get to live a normal life, a charmed life and others can get fucked up for no rhyme or reason and it be okay. What God does that... What God is like, "Yikes, you got fucked up huh? Welp, shit happens! See you when I see you.'," shrugs.

Are you kidding me...aren't you freaking God????

TRANSFORMED

Be careful what you ask for…you just might get it.

A couple of weeks later after not finishing that course, I went to sleep like I always do, thinking, "Oh, hope I wake up," and something happened. An experience occurred that changed the entire trajectory of my life. Some people will say it was a dream, some may say a visitation, truly I don't know what to call it, but I do know it was real. I found myself in this giant room with a female dressed all in white, with long dark hair, and there were huge TV screens that covered the wall as far as I could see, standing at what looked like a control board, she said calmly, "She wants to know if she could change events in her life, would things have turned out differently than where they are right now."

I'm confused as hell because I had no idea who she was talking to until I looked over to the right and it was a man with dark, curly hair sitting there, legs crossed, and he answered, "We'll allow her to do so." She looks at me and says "Okay, take the helm." I looked up at those screens and saw all the events of my life.

Whoa, what the fu…!

She said, "You can take out what you want to take out and you can rearrange what you want to rearrange." I said, "Okay", and I did that and ended up in the same damn spot I was in right now.

PSA: I know you all are wondering what they looked like or what ethnicity they were so I will indulge. They both looked like everyone. Those beings could literally stand next to every ethnicity and blend in...it was crazy! And I felt their power, but they were so loving, patient, and gentle with me.

Okay back to our regularly scheduled programming...

Now I don't know how many times I did it, but each time I rearranged the events of my life, I would end up in the same position. And with each turn, I got more and more frustrated. I would look at the man and he would gently say, "If you want to do it again, go ahead."

Not one time did either of them get frustrated or upset with how many times I went through the motions. They were very, very loving, like, they could sit there for an eternity, if that's what it was going to take. And like I said, I don't know how many times I did it, but finally I turned to him frustrated and said, "I don't understand. I keep coming back to the same place. Why?

That's when he said, "Because we needed you to experience all of the things that you went through, and the reason why you went through them is to fashion you into the person that you are today to do what we need you to do."

TRANSFORMED

BOOM!

As soon as he said that his powerful voice echoed in my head and my eyes popped open and I was back in my bed. I jumped out of bed. Reminder, I am more than 400 pounds, but I **literally** leaped out of bed, and I was completely on fire. My entire body was hot, and I was wide awake. I began pacing around the room thinking what in the world just happened. Where did I just go? I can't even unpack this right now because I think I had two hours left before I had to get up to go to work. I climbed back into bed and fell immediately back to sleep.

I woke up to the sound of my alarm, showered, and dressed all on autopilot. When I got in the car to take that long trip to the office, I started processing everything that happened. That's when it hit me like a lightning bolt! I experienced God in the duality of male and female. Which makes sense if they were going to get through to me, I would have to feel comfortable and at ease. I started crying. I realized that I finally got my why. Not only did I get the why, but God saw fit to take the time to bring me there, little ol' Nia Danielle from Newark, New Jersey, from one little ass planet in one solar system of who knows how many, to them in forms that were comfortable for me, to tell me in person. The magnitude of that changed me forever. Whenever I think about that, even right now as I'm writing this, I get overwhelmed with emotion.

That was the first time I truly felt God's love and I realized I was worthy of it.

With this newfound sense of purpose, (which is ironic because my name means purpose) I sat in that car and talked to God. I mean really had a conversation and it went something like, "Okay, so what is it that I need to do? And in having such an important mission, help me because I can't do whatever it is in my present physical state. I need to change my life, I want to change my entire life, and I want to make a deal with you all. I want to lose weight once and for all. You back me up on this and I will go balls to the wall. I will do whatever I can, I will give it my all. This is going to be my last try, but I will give everything that I have to this thing, and if it doesn't work out, take me. But if it does work out, and I lose this weight, I promise to never put myself in this position again. I'll do what it takes. Just give me the reset button I need, and I'll never waste it."

In November 2015, I decided to go forward with weight loss surgery. The moment the thought crossed my mind, it sat well with my soul, and I knew that was supposed to be my path regardless of what anybody had to say. I felt settled in a way that felt like something clicked in my being. IT CLICKED!!! I've always heard about instances where people say they felt a click when something just felt right. I felt it a few times when I decided to go to Art school and then when I received the internship at WGNX, but I never felt it whenever I decided to lose weight...until now.

I told a core group of people in my life, mind you, I told them this is what I was doing. I didn't ask for their opinion or for them to weigh in on the decision, (no pun intended but that was cute). I only told them because I wanted them to support me in my journey, I knew I would need a good support system. I was very strategic in who I asked because those who couldn't support me wouldn't be in my inner circle.

They all agreed and of course, there was apprehension about the whole procedure in general, however, they understood that the decision I believed was best for me and this is what I was going to do, so they were behind me 100%. I scheduled an appointment to attend the mandatory seminar required for entry into the weight loss surgery program, and I began my final weight loss journey.

CHAPTER 5

Here's The Skinny...

What WLS is and How to Get It

So here comes the good part, this is the meat and potatoes for all those people who are contemplating weight loss surgery (WLS) and want to know what to do. I want to reiterate that this was the process that I had to go through to get approved at that time. Your process may vary slightly depending on what your qualification requirements are for your insurance company. Some of this may bore you folks who are not going to go through this, but I encourage you to read it anyway. I say that because the biggest misconception is that it is sooo easy to get any weight loss surgery and we are truly taking the easy way out. Ha! I wish that was the case but it's not. It may be easier if you are paying out-of-pocket completely, but if you are dealing with insurance…you're jumping through hoops to get the outcome you desire.

And…you never know where I'm going to drop some gems or a juicy story and skipping parts will cause you to miss out. Then, when someone asks you about a part in the book, you will have to fake it like you remember and try to go back to find it!

When I started my journey, I was required to attend a two-hour seminar, in which they showed a video advising about obesity and then they gave a brief overview of their program and discussed the next steps if you have decided to move forward with the weight loss surgery route.

Weight loss surgery costs a pretty penny so having insurance, great insurance is optimal. In my situation, because I had the insurance that I had, my overall out-of-pocket for the weight loss surgery was whatever the maximum out-of-pocket expense for that year, including paying co-pays, deductibles, and and other related costs. I was grateful that my company had opted to cover weight loss surgery because some companies do not, and without insurance, the cost can run you upwards of $30,000, depending on what kind of surgery you want to have, whether your procedure is the sleeve, the gastric, or the Duodenal Switch that I received. Regardless, if you must pay out-of-pocket, that is quite a bit of money for the average person. There are also some finance options if you don't have insurance coverage, but the terms are determined by your credit score and any other factors the financial institutions require.

Plus, you must factor in other expenses not covered by insurance such as the required nutrition class. I also had to pay for the psyche evaluation, and if necessary, you may have to pay for the therapy if you don't have insurance. Post-surgery, you will have to pay for your subsequent visits back to the doctor, you may have to pay for your comprehensive blood panel, depending upon your insurance, which tells you where you are as far as your vitamins and minerals, and your nutrition on the inside, and you have to keep that up because you will be going to the doctor every month, then every quarter, and then every six months and then yearly for check-ins. You also must be mindful that you may or may not have complications. I happened to develop pancreatitis about a month after surgery, so I had to be hospitalized.

Once you have the surgery you also should make sure that you have money for your multivitamins and any other special vitamins you may need, again, you will be on multi-vitamins for life.

Okay, moving on...

When I first went to my first seminar, I went through that whole two-hour presentation, and I provided my insurance information to schedule my medical evaluations for assessing my physical condition and what course of action we needed to take. This was the beginning of November, and I was so excited that I was on my way to having this surgery! This is going to be so easy and smooth, I have God/Goddess on my side, so I am WINNING!

I began the tedious approval process; I met with the doctor and weighed in, they took my vitals and registered me into the system. What they didn't know was that I could hear them discussing my case and I heard the doctor say I was a candidate, but they didn't even know how much I weigh since the scale only goes to 400 hundred pounds. Well, damn. In retrospect, it almost sounded like he didn't want to do it. I was confused and embarrassed because aren't these supposed to be the team dedicated to people like me trying to change my life?

About two weeks later, I got a phone call from the finance office, informing me that the program at the hospital wasn't covered by my insurance, so unfortunately, I couldn't continue with their team. I was shocked and she went further to tell me that they didn't have any further information and that I should contact my insurance provider to have them make a recommendation on what bariatric team was covered in my plan.

DAMN, so much for easy.

So, I thought that meant that I had to just get my testing done at the approved facility, and that's when she burst my bubble and said I would probably have to start all over again with the two-hour seminar.

FUCK!!!! You've got to be kidding me!?!?!

I recall talking to one of my friends, I was just so upset and discouraged. Are you serious? I'm already three weeks in, and I had to start all over? Plus, it takes a while to get into a seminar as they are not held every day or even every week. She asked me what I was gonna do. I thought back to that pact I made and dug in. You know what, I don't give a damn if I needed to start over. I'm just gonna start over and work much harder to speed up the timeline because I already wasted three weeks.

PSA: Sometimes, obstacles are put in your path to test you, to see just how committed you are to whatever it is you're doing. It's not designed to prevent you from achieving your goal, it's placed there to show you just what you are made of.

I contacted my insurance provider directly and was able to get an approved facility from them and scheduled my slot for the seminar. In the meantime, I took the advice of one of my friends and I reached out to a couple of other associates that I knew had the surgery. I wanted to get firsthand experience on what to expect regarding the process and what kind of timeline I was looking at. Each one had a different surgery, but they all said the same thing, it would be at least six months to a year before I would receive my cut date, based on the stringent criteria involved.

I know myself better than anyone on this planet, so I know for a fact that I do not have the patience to go through a year-long process before I can even get the surgery. Up until this point, I would concede that I didn't have the willpower, nor did I feel that I had that kind of time. For me, I was so used to the yo-yo dieting, where progress was made up to a certain point, and then all of a sudden something happens and you're right back where you started with more weight. So, I couldn't imagine myself having to maintain whatever plan they were going to have me do for up to a year before I could even get a date. That's not happening. I told each of them that I was not going to wait that long and that I would have my surgery date before the first quarter of 2016 was over.

They thought it was impossible as we were in the latter part of November already. They said it was unprecedented and they had never seen or heard anybody do it in under six months.

They don't know Me.

I attended the seminar, where I met my future bariatric surgeon, and he looked like he could be one of the 12 apostles, I promise you, he does. Anyway, I'm going through the two-hour seminar, and this time I don't know what it was, but I was really, really listening.

Number one, I did not realize that obesity is an epidemic in America, the CDC has labeled it an epidemic, which is the reason why more and more insurance companies are covering weight loss surgery because it's literally an epidemic that no one is talking about.

Number two, once you reach a certain BMI, there's a 2% chance someone who was morbidly obese will be able to get down to a normal size on their own without any surgeries. I let that sink in for a minute and I felt relief because I realized it's not just me, it's a whole bunch of overweight people running around here trying very, very hard to achieve this goal, and it's just not working. The odds are literally stacked against us, and no, it's not for lack of trying, it's not because we are lazy or greedy, it is almost an impossible task. Why? Because after a certain BMI is reached, your body considers that normal. When you go into dieting, it'll let go of the first 20, 25 pounds, 30 at the most, after that, your body is so smart that it feels like it's starving. It thinks it's losing our factory setting, so it starts retaining everything you eat, triggering cravings to make you get that weight back on because it's going into self-preservation mode.

Once you fall off the wagon and start gaining weight, you will not only gain the weight back that you lost, but your body will add a few insurance pounds, just in case you become foolish enough in the future to put its factory setting in jeopardy again.

And now you really feel like a failure.

You forget the whole process until you gain a new resolve, and then you start that cycle over again, you lose 20 pounds, you gain 25 more, and you just keep doing that over and over and over again. For a lot of us, that cycle is not gonna end, you're just gonna get bigger and bigger. Again, I'm not talking about everybody. Some people have these wonderful success stories, because I have heard them in the past when I was a big girl, about how something in their brain just clicked and they got in that gym and they worked hard and they changed their eating habits, and they lost all that weight, and now they're wonderful and living a healthy fit lifestyle. Kudos to them! But that shit was not my story, not my story at all, and it's not quite a few people's stories. That endgame wasn't going to be my road to success and that was okay because again, there is more than one way to get to ten.

At the end of the seminar, I introduced myself to the bariatric surgeon, and he looked kindly at me and said, "Yes, I can tell right away, even before meeting you, that you qualify for surgery." He proceeded to ask me how much I weighed, and I told him. He advised me immediately that he would not perform any surgery until I got my BMI down below 60. I was confused and asked him wasn't that the reason why I was getting the surgery. He stated he would not operate past a certain BMI because of the health risks, so it's a must that I get to that number.

He asked if I had a primary care physician and when I said no, he referred me to the Primary Care Physician that he works closely with regarding his bariatric patients. He then advised that his team would schedule an appointment to become part of their program. He then gave me the information to set up an appointment with my new PCP, so we can begin to get this process started. He shook my hand and said, "Welcome." At that moment, I felt like this time was different. I dare to say it might just happen.

And that's when it happened, a feeling settled over me. I was hearing all these years about how shit clicks in your brain, and you just change at that moment, something in me clicked and I thought, "This just might be it... " All of that dreaming and daydreaming and fantasizing about what I would look like small, the life I would live small, my day-to-day activities, and all those little crazy-assed daydreams. It might actually become a reality. Like, what if I do lose this weight, for real? What if this man really wants to help me? All of this played out in my head at that moment.

I made an appointment with his assistant, who took my insurance information (within a couple of days it came back that it was approved, so there were no setbacks this time). When I arrived, I was weighed in on a proper scale, then they took my blood to test all of my levels to determine how I would fare with the procedure. Then he and I sat down and had a real conversation about my current weight and my goals, which would determine which procedure we agreed would be the most optimal for me. We chose to move forward with the Duodenal Switch procedure due to how much weight I wanted to lose versus the time after the procedure you have before your body begins to plateau.

PSA: All your levels should be tested as far as your vitamins, minerals, and general health concerns. You should be checked for diabetes, anemia, hypertension, or anything that would trigger a snag in the process.

Based on your insurance, you'll have different requirements to meet to qualify for the surgery. I didn't have to go to a cardiologist based on my history, but I did have to go to the pulmonologist because I snore very loudly and I was diagnosed with sleep apnea a long time ago, so I had to do another sleep study, which they discovered I had severe sleep apnea.

As a matter of fact, they said that it was probably one of the worst cases they had seen because I stopped breathing so many times in an hour, they almost couldn't count. It makes sense now why I was always so damn tired, and I could fall asleep on a dime. I fell asleep at my desk so randomly that I thought I was developing narcolepsy, but it was because I didn't get quality sleep. I think they advised within the 60-minute time frame, I stopped breathing more than 20 times when my brain had to wake me up like, "Don't die," I never got into the deep rem state, which is why I was always fatigued. Thus, causing me to drink so much caffeine. After they did the sleep study, I was put on a little machine, which is so annoying and totally not sexy. But I immediately felt a difference in my sleep patterns and definitely felt more rested. I was advised that bringing that machine with me to the hospital was mandatory because going under anesthesia with sleep apnea is dangerous.

The real Vitamin D.

My blood panel came back from the lab, and I have to say that I am so grateful for him and I'm so angry at every other doctor because he was the only one who told me that my iron levels were very low, and I had to start taking iron pills. I have been to the doctor's before, and nobody said anything. Also, my vitamin D levels were dangerously low, I was severely vitamin D deficient, and had to be prescribed vitamin D and I started taking them immediately. I don't know what the number is, but if the minimum level is twenty-seven, then mine was around nine.

I didn't realize it was that bad and serious. What I didn't know was that you need vitamin D in your system to battle a heart attack. With the level that I had, if I was to in fact have a heart attack, my chances of survival at that time were zero. ZERO!

That's when I started researching and realized a lot of melanite people are Vitamin D deficient and don't know it, and that got me thinking, if a lot of black people are vitamin D deficient, that might contribute to why a lot of black people don't survive heart attacks. Why isn't this common knowledge and why isn't testing our vitamin D levels on a regular part of routine wellness check-ups? I'm going to leave that right there… aside from the anemia and vitamin D issue, everything else came back peachy.

PSA: People, especially melanite people, please make sure you tell your doctor to check your vitamin D levels to ensure you are good.

I told you I was a woman on a mission, so I was blazing through the checklist of requirements the insurance provider and my bariatric surgeon gave me:

Mandatory nutrition class: Aced it, passed the test BOOM!

Pulmonologist: Completed the sleep study, received, and used the machine check!

Blood work: Done. Taking the prescribed meds, Oh yeah!

Primary care physician appointment: I met with the doctor, and she checked all my vitals, everything was good, and she advised we were going to work on losing weight to get the BMI down. She prescribed medication that promotes weight loss, and I changed my eating habits and incorporated more water. Awesome!

I'm thinking, alright, cool. I'm good, I'm cooking with grease at this point. By that time, this was towards the end of December, and I was performing exceptionally well and making a mark so by January, I'll have a cut date.

Storytime:

Remember when I said sometimes, Source will throw a curveball in your path to test your commitment? Well sometimes, you are also thrown a curveball to completely confirm your decision. This happened to me on December 26th, 2015, a date I will never forget. Of course, it was the day after Christmas, when I visited one of my besties, Adriane, to drop off gifts. I was also going to see a good friend of mine on that side of town who was here for the holidays. Adriane was leaving to meet up with family and so I had a couple of hours to kill and decided to go to the movies, to pass the time (I am a big, big, big, movie-goer to this day. It's one of my favorite pastimes). I arrived at the mall, parked, and walked to the side where the theater entrance was located, nothing unusual. I entered the theater, where the entire front was all glass doors, and proceeded to stand in line with the rest of the patrons, to purchase a ticket.

Suddenly, we heard gunshots. Everyone in the theater starts running for cover, including me. I've been to this theater a hundred times, so I know the layout like the back of my hand, so within a split second I knew I wasn't going to make it across the floor to where the theaters were to be able to hide or exit through those back doors. I wasn't even going to make it to the bathrooms, but I also didn't want to get trapped there as we didn't know if the shooter was going to come in here or what was going on. I was only able to get to the ticket counter and crouch behind there with an elderly couple. I peeked and saw the shooter traveling past the theater, gun out and shooting. I was so terrified. But also, I was so angry at myself because even though I knew the best way out, I couldn't physically move fast enough to execute the plan in my head.

For a long couple of hours, we were told to stay in the theater until the entire perimeter was secured. Later, we discovered the shooting wasn't random as it began as an altercation between some teens in the mall. Still, at that time we didn't know if he was coming in or whoever he was targeting, was going to run for cover here, and bring him in as well.

But that entire horrific ordeal made me think about just how much of a liability I was at this weight. I was at the point where I couldn't save myself and I would possibly put other people I loved in danger if I was with them because I knew someone like my brother wouldn't want to leave me behind. Honestly, I wasn't interested in being left behind like the wounded person in the movie who gives their life to save others by taking the detonator and sacrifices themselves for the greater good. I'm a Capricorn, we don't even like the greater good like that!

Hell no, in a movie like 300, I wanted to be in the 301+ count that would be telling the story about the brave 300 that didn't make it, but we will remember them always. This too, made me realize I don't want to die. I don't want to just exist.

I want to live.

It's now 2016, I'm on schedule with all my appointments. Everything was cool physically, so I was confident that the hardest part was over, but there was one more requirement to complete. The psyche evaluation. Hey, no problem I'm not that crazy, so an appointment was scheduled. And that's when I was gobsmacked with another plot twist.

I received my referral to a psychologist, and I was going to my appointment. He explains the test is a series of questions, which I will need to answer to the best of my ability, after which he will review it and we will discuss the results. Not a problem. I'm very confident in my ability to take assessment tests as I always score in the top percentile, so this shouldn't be any different. After the first few questions, I started to waiver, my spidey sense was going off. It was something about these answers that I had to give; if I answered truthfully, and I didn't want to lie because there were some tricky interrogation-type questions in this evaluation that I felt would be incriminating.

For example, do you know the character assessment tests you take for certain jobs, and they ask you the same question but in a different way to see if you are consistent and honest? The first question would read, "Would you ever take a pencil?" Then two pages down the line they ask, "Would you ever remove a pencil from the facility?" that's still asking if you would steal a pencil, it's just worded differently...

That's how the evaluation started to feel. If I started lying now, he's going to know, so I kept going, and the more I answered those questions, the more I started to think...Bitch, I think you failed this test. Once I completed the test and he completed the review, he asked me to sit down so we could discuss his assessment.

I will say...when I first walked in the doors, I liked this shrink and I'd never seen a psychologist who was such a laid-back hippie. He looked like he took a trip to Woodstock and just came back. He cracked me up and he was cool, and his office was all vibed out - he was from California, so that explained it. That's why I thought initially that I was a shoo-in to pass. I mean he had beaded hangings and a Lil Buddha, so I was **sure** I was gonna pass - he was about peace and love and probably smoked weed, so I'm good!

NOT. AT. ALL.

I'm sitting across from him, and he begins with, "Soo..." and it was at that moment that I knew I failed. I said, "I failed it." He tried to make me feel better by telling me that there's no such thing as passing or failing. I then asked him if he was going to approve of me being mentally able to get the surgery. He said no and so to me, that's a failure.

Did I mention that I hate this guy?

He went on to say that he wanted me to succeed. His exact words were, "There is something about you that makes me want you to succeed in this, and I would do you a disservice if I just say, or stamp yes, go ahead and give her the surgery," he said. "I promise you, if I told you yes right now, based on your answers, based on your triggers, you'll get the surgery. It may be successful for the first year or so, but I promise you... In five years, you'll be right back when you started physically, because for you, it's not a physical thing, it's a mental and emotional thing. I can tell the way you're answering your questions, you don't even eat a lot of your calories, you drink your calories. So, it's not even about an eating issue, it's something else going on there, and I can't in good conscience, as you say, 'pass you', because I already know what that outcome is gonna be." He paused and then said, "so, I'm not saying no. I'm saying you need further evaluation, and I think that therapy is the answer. I have a few recommendations for therapists that will help you and they will determine when you are ready, for the surgery to be successful."

Therapy!?!?!

This muthafucka said therapy. You know black people don't go to therapy. Where do black people go to... Jesus which is…. I'm not even going there as that is another story for another book. So now I've got to Jedi mind trick this new therapist into approving me. Okay. Whatever I gotta do, I'm gonna do it.

Commence with the shrinking.

Meanwhile, back at the ranch, I'm trying to lose that weight to get my BMI down to the required number for my bariatric surgeon to sign off on the surgery. Right now, I am literally off the charts. I wasn't in the category of morbid obesity, I was in the next category, the one that wasn't even on the paper, he had to physically tell me I was in the extreme morbid obese category. I wasn't aware a category like that even existed.

The BMI categories go like this:

underweight - less than 18.5

healthy weight - 18.5 - 24.9

overweight obese - 30.0 - 39.9

morbid obesity - over 40

extreme morbid obesity - off the grid or over 60

So, for him to do the surgery, I had to get to a certain BMI which I believe is max under 60. Currently, I was a little over 400 pounds, and my BMI was 66, so I had to lose at least thirty pounds to qualify and maintain it up until the surgery date.

As a requirement, my nutritionist had me keep a food diary. During my follow-up session, he said the same thing the psychologist stated. I was eating more calories than I drank, and I wasn't consuming what my physical weight was displaying.

A freaking conspiracy I tell ya.

TRANSFORMED

I started changing my eating habits to less fried and fast food. I drank less sugary beverages and started drinking more water and taking the meds my doctor prescribed. I was walking on the treadmill with some ladies at work at the local gym. I was like, yeah, I'm gonna do this. The first 10 pounds came off. Five more pounds came off. Yes! Then, right when I started therapy, the weight loss stopped.

I chose a black woman as my therapist. Personally, I felt like I could be more comfortable during this session because, in my mind, I think I would only need to convince her of my plight. So here we go, and my Jedi mind trick must be on point because you know we see right through each other. As I sat down with her, I began to rethink my decision. I could've gotten over easily on anyone else other than a black woman. But at the same time, I didn't get past the hippie white therapist. Either way, it's too late, I am here.

This is a showdown - at least, in my head, as I am sitting across from her in our first session.

She starts off with, "You don't wanna be here, do you?"

Whoa, okay. She gets it…maybe we are on the same page.

I said, "Nope, I sure don't... I'm ready for the surgery, I don't understand why I failed the test." She started on that whole not passing or failing thing and I stopped her and told her to please spare me the lesson on pass or fail because I was sitting here due to the fact I failed. She laughed and said, "Okay, you failed but what are we going to do about it?"

Is she a Virgo? This is something my bestie Adriane has said verbatim!

What do I want to do about it? I honestly didn't know exactly how to answer that. What I did know is that I wanted to do whatever it took to get approval from all parties involved. She told me that I needed to be evaluated for about six weeks and around the end she would give her recommendation to the surgeon on whether I was a prime candidate for a successful outcome. It's already January, so six weeks will put me well into February, maybe even early March and that would cut close to my deadline.

Crap, I knew I wasn't going to be able to get over this sister, so now I went straight into negotiations mode. I'm a Capricorn, the goat, the climber, and therefore relentless in my pursuit of what I want.

Time to wheel and deal. So, I used the card I knew she would respond to: **HONESTY**.

I flat out told her that I needed to get this surgery by the end of this quarter because I have a track record of giving up after a period without seeing the results I want, or my body turning on me and putting the weight back on. I made her an offer that I would continue to come to therapy for at least six months to a year after my surgery and do the work if she would pass me.

She said she couldn't commit to that right now, but we'll talk about it at the end of these next six weeks. I was totally going to have to do the work.

As much as I hated that little hippie doctor because I really did, I hated him at that moment, and I kind of really hated my new therapist, but they made the best decision for me. He was absolutely correct, had I gotten my way and he pushed me through like the no child left behind initiative, I probably wouldn't be sitting here writing this book. I'd probably have gained my weight back like so many others that I know, because there was a lot of shit that I unearthed in therapy which I had no idea was an issue. Things I never thought that I would have to unpack, and now, I had no choice but to unpack it, but I'll talk about that in the next chapter.

I started my therapeutic journey, and I was completely raw, honest, and even began to look forward to the sessions. By the fourth week, she told me that she believed I was in the right frame of mind to have the surgery!

Oh, Happy Day!

She stipulated that I continue to see her at least a few weeks post-op to ensure that I can cope with the aftermath of surgery mentally. Like my first psychologist, this therapist also wanted me to win. I agreed because in all honesty, I wanted to continue as it was helping me in so many ways not just with my weight, but with some of the personal conflicts I had or was having, and she was there to listen without judgment. I think everyone would benefit from an unbiased person trained to listen and aid you in doing your shadow work.

Now, you would think that I was good, right? Because the pulmonologist signed off on me, the therapist had now signed off on me, my bloodwork was stable. The only person that was stopping me at this point was me. Why? Because of my weight loss plateauing, I could not get past that 15-20 pound mark, and now it started to creep back up again. I had an appointment to see My PCP and document my weight loss. Of course, I already knew I still was not at the goal. She stated she was giving me another 90 days and then come back for another office visit to check my progress.

Absolutely not.

I asked her how much weight I would need to lose to get to the desired under-60 BMI. She advised I would need to lose at least 15 pounds or so, so give it a couple of more months and then we will check in. I knew I didn't have a couple of months; I was in a do-or-die mode…balls to the wall. She must have read the look on my face because she said if, at any point, I felt I had reached the necessary weight for the surgery, I should call her, and she would have them squeeze me in the same day.

The next day I reached out to my nutritionist. I told him about the meds I was on and how I am now stagnant with losing the last 15 pounds to qualify for the surgery. I wanted to know if there was anything he could further recommend getting me to my goal. He advised If I really wanted to get real, it's gonna be hard, but he emailed the criteria to get me there: no sugar, no dairy, no starches. All you're gonna eat Is grilled lean meat, preferably fish or chicken, and grilled vegetables.

Breakfast and lunch consist of protein drinks, and I'm not talking about the good kind in the stores that everybody loves to drink. No, no, I'm talking about the big liquid kind that looked like colored water and it's like 40 ounces of this stupid shit. I had to drink one for each meal because I had to get my protein in as that was all that mattered, not taste. I had to drink eight glasses of water. No snacks, I could drink tea and coffee, but without any cream or sugar. Dinner consisted of grilled meat and veggies in the proper portions he taught in the nutrition class. That will boost my metabolism and I'll be able to lose weight.

That's it.

This was the middle of March 2016, and my personal deadline was looming dangerously ahead, so I did it, and I was laser focused. Now, mind you, again, the universe has a funny way of testing your willpower because the entire time that I was doing the meal plan, all of a sudden, the office had all kinds of celebrations that consisted of goodies and treats, free breakfast today, free catered lunch next day. Hey, we got some clients that came into the office and decided to buy lunch. Free food was everywhere. But I didn't give a damn. All I kept saying in my head was "I'm not wavering, I'm not wavering, I'm not wavering." I would sit at my desk and drink my little shakes and water, and the girls around me told me that I was inspiring them not to indulge.

They had never seen anyone with that much willpower in the face of all this food temptation. Honestly, I had never seen **myself** with that much willpower in my life. This time was different, this time I was focused because I made a promise to myself and God/Goddess that I was going to give 100%, and that's what the hell I'm doing. I did that for a solid week. I started on Thursday and continued until the following Friday; I woke up with the feeling that I had reached my goal. I called the doctor's office, and they advised me to just come in at the last appointment just as the doctor promised.

TRANSFORMED

I skipped my lunch hour and drove to the office. I had on typical work clothes but underneath I wore a sports bra and biker shorts because I was going to get as close to naked as possible as every stitch of clothing you wear weighs something!

So, as they are calling me to the back, I see the doctor, and she smiles at me with a kind of sadness. I knew she didn't want to see me devastated when the scale didn't give the proper number for her to provide the approval letter to my surgeon.

Once I got back, the ladies at the counter greeted me, they all knew me and knew my story. There was one new person who happened to have my chart and he stated that we are going to first weigh you. I happily replied, "That's why I am here!" And everyone laughed. Then they really started laughing when I told him to hold on while I removed my shoes, shirt, and skirt. This was serious business and by now I was getting nervous. What if I didn't make it? What if I gained instead of lost? Do I have it in me to keep going?

I stepped on that scale, and it seemed like all the ladies were holding their breath.

I was holding my breath as the digital reader tried to settle on a number. When it did, I couldn't believe it.

I lost 19 pounds. In just seven days.

When the guy read the weight and said I dropped 19 pounds, the entire room erupted in cheers. It was surreal, I kept blinking and repeating to myself, "I did it."

That's when my PCP came down the hall and asked what happened. The medical assistant told her my weight, and she said, "Oh my God, you did it!" When I tell you she was jumping up and down, got teary-eyed, exclaiming that she couldn't believe it and that she'd never seen anybody drop 19 pounds in seven days. She advised me to take my things and get dressed in the room as she was writing the letter and sending it straight to the surgeon's office. She returned to the room and said that I was such an inspiration and when she first saw me her heart sank because she cared so much and didn't want to disappoint me again. She told me she had called my surgeon and told him the good news and the approval paperwork was confirmed and will be received at his office, so they will reach out regarding the next steps. She hugged me and told me that she couldn't wait to see my transformation once I had the surgery.

I think two days later when I was at work, I got that call. They scheduled my pre-op date, based on the projected surgery date they scheduled:

April 12, 2016.

And there it is, and I was like, goddamn, I did it!

TRANSFORMED

From November 2015, the first time I attended my very first seminar, to my surgery date April 12, 2016, is around five months. I set the goal to receive my cut date by the end of the first quarter and I did. Nobody thought I was gonna be able to do that in under a year, but I did it in under six months and I was and still damn proud of myself.

I always had fantasies of being small, I would daydream about myself, in my desired size. To me, it wasn't visualization, it was more like it was a fantasy because I wanted it so badly, but I didn't really believe that I would ever get there, so I kind of escaped into that fantastical world where I was dare I say 150 pounds, which I literally felt like, I'll probably never get there. If I can get to 200 pounds, I can safely go on to glory and be happy about it, but in a perfect world, I'd be 150 pounds and sexy and I'll be able to wear this or that because I love fashion, I love creating new looks for myself.

My fantasy life, that was my real world, and a lot of times I would fantasize, or daydream way more than I would be aware and experiencing my real life. I couldn't wait to fantasize. I **lived** in that world, and I know that sounds crazy, but I literally existed in this world, but I lived in that world. I don't know if a whole lot of people will understand what I'm saying, but if you know you know.

I existed in this world all day, as I woke up, ate breakfast, went to work, came home, watched TV, maybe talked to friends, dealt with my family life, went to bed to wake up and do it all over again. But when I was in that fantasy world, I traveled freely, went to parties and fine dining, dressed the way I wanted, had lovers, and truly lived another life.

So, when I got to that point where I met my bariatric surgeon, and I said something clicked. It clicked like, hey, can I bring that fantasy out and make it a reality? It will no longer be a fantasy, that will be my reality, and this reality will no longer be real to me, that it would be but a long-ago dream. That is what caused me to catch my breath like I might actually be able to live full-time in that world and make that world my world, and that is what was so profound to me that I'll always remember that moment because that was the moment that changed my life.

I made the most important decision with myself and how I see God/Goddess and I felt truly that we were all working collectively, to conspire in my favor to conjure my fantasy timeline into my actual timeline. I had hoped, prayed, and visualized me stepping into that world for good. Only in my wildest dreams did I think that I could create a bridge that would allow me to cross from one world to the next, but we did.

TRANSFORMED

And I am walking across that bridge.

CHAPTER 6

Exit The Warrior And Enter The Goddess

Surgery, here we go...

Okay, so I got my surgery date, which was April 12, 2016.

That's when shit got real because it's here, and once I do it, there's no turning back, no more excuses. The time came when I had to go through my pre-op appointment, which was a day or two before the surgery, and of course, they recorded all my vitals just as confirmation that everything was still good to go. I met with the anesthesiologist, and he explained what was going to happen with his side of things. Prior to that, I had submitted my request for short-term disability because I was going to be out recovering for about 4-6 weeks. Since weight loss surgery is covered by insurance, my STD was also covered. Plus, I received so much positive support from the leaders at my job as well as my colleagues. Everyone knew what was going on and was cheering me on the entire time. Leadership made sure I had coverage while I was gone, so I had no worries, the folks that I supported in my role were covered.

Early Tuesday morning, I headed to the airport to pick up my mom flying in from Florida. That day, my phone was flooded with well wishes from family, friends, and co-workers. We arrived at the hospital and got all checked in. My niece Amaris wanted to be there, so her mom dropped her off as well and two of my besties, Adriane and Tina also came to the hospital. I just remember thinking, as we're sitting there and they're taking my vitals, hooking me up to the IVs and I'm lying in the private hospital room, chatting with my mom that in a few short hours, things will never be the same.

Now, the next thing I know, my mom leaves for a while, and then she and my friends return with Chick-fil-A. Are you kidding me!?!? I hadn't eaten solid food in two days, because I had to prep my body. Let me explain that this whole 'last meal' the day before you have surgery is a myth if you are following the path the doctor lays out. You're supposed to prep your body for two days, which means you're off of solid foods and you will be on liquids, in order to clean out your system and shrink your liver to make the surgery optimal, and I was a by-the-book Betty. Everything My surgeon told me to do, I did it, no cheating, no cutting corners, none of that nonsense.

It's funny now but when these wonderful human beings I call family, unwittingly showed up in my room with those bags full of tasty chicken biscuits and hash rounds, I wanted to smack each and every one of them! I had two words for them, "Get Out!" LOL! They hurried up and scurried their asses out of my room and into the main waiting area.

Next thing I know, the nurse enters my room and says, "Alright, it's time."

It is time.

They wheeled me out of the room and headed to the OR. As I was passing through the corridors of the hospital, I said goodbye to the old Nia. She's literally going to die today, and the new Nia is going to emerge when I come out of this surgery. I felt the gravity of that, and a certain wistfulness set in because I've been with this version of myself all my life. She was a warrior, and she protected me through a lot of tough situations. But now, I was ready for her to lay down and allow the goddess to blossom. The last thing that I remember was thinking, "Goodbye warrior Nia, you served me well, love you," and then I was out.

I didn't have any complications that might occur during these types of surgeries. The surgeon stated the procedure went perfectly, as my body was in such pristine condition internally. Everything was perfect, I was flawlessly cleaned out... bonafide textbook. He said he had not seen someone so clean and pristine internally, I absolutely did my job. Afterwards, I woke up to such excruciating pain. I started dry heaving which progressed to vomiting bile and it was painful. The doctor stayed in recovery with me and would not let me go to my room because he didn't want me to get there and then during an episode, rupture something on the inside, and they would have to rush me back to the OR. He kept me there for a while until he felt I was good enough to journey upstairs.

If this was the new Nia being born...these were some hellafied labor pains.

I was supposed to stay in recovery for about 45 minutes after the surgery, and the surgery was only for an hour, so my family and I were looking at about 2 ½ hours, max. The surgery lasted during the allotted time, but I think I stayed in recovery for a couple of hours because they kept sending word to my family that I was okay, but they needed to keep me, to watch me because I was having some slight issues. By that time, a crowd of friends and family had gathered at the hospital.

Finally, I was able to be moved to my room, and it was kind of foggy, but I remember coming down the corridor and seeing the vast group of people waiting for me, I couldn't make out everybody because I was in such pain, and at that moment, I had major buyer's remorse. I was thinking, "I don't know why I did this... I shouldn't have done this, Lord, I shouldn't have done this." As I approached the room, everybody began greeting me and I recall waving back at them, I was so overwhelmed with the pain, and I didn't want to scare them, but I was about to lose it... I was wheeled into the room, and they were starting to file in, but the nurse must have seen the look on my face because she asked if I needed a minute before they came in and I nodded, so the only person she let in was my mom. She advised everyone else to give them a few minutes to get me settled in and gently closed the door.

As soon as the door was shut, I immediately started crying. I was in so much pain. My mom was trying to comfort me by telling me it was going to be okay. The nurses were encouraging me and advising me this was only temporary, and that it would get better by the hour. Then they told me about the lovely, blessed morphine button. Aaaahh, my new and much-needed best friend.

I immediately grabbed the button, but they advised me not to press it until I saw my visitors because I would go dark instantly. One of the nurses opened the door and everybody came and gave their well wishes, asked how I was doing, and that they were proud of me. I remember nodding, smiling, telling them I was good, and giving them the thumbs up. As they left, I pressed that button and would not let go. Only a certain amount of morphine is going to be released each time, but I held onto that button as if I could get it to operate like a drip! Sweet unconscious bliss soon followed. Then I woke up with the pain all over again, not remembering the button, so my mom had to gently remind me to press it.

They released me the evening of the following day because you must walk, and you have to urinate in order to be discharged. Again, I am not going to lie... I was in some serious pain. Part of it was, that I didn't realize because I had the Loop DS, my stomach was cut down to the size of an egg and sat right in the middle of my breasts and I wasn't quite used to having my stomach where it was located, which normally your stomach is kind of like diagonal across your body a little bit. Now, my egg-sized stomach literally sat in the middle of my cleavage, right where my bra rests. I remember whenever I wore bras, I had to lift my bra up because the pressure from the weight of my breasts would press down and make me nauseous. Sometimes people would see me try to discreetly lift the center of the bra to relieve the pressure because it affected me well after I hit my goal weight.

Then I noticed that every few hours I would have sharp pains in that area. I didn't recognize the feeling, or where it was coming from, and I think by the third day of being baffled by this pain coming every two to three hours something in my head said, Are you hungry? Is this what the new hunger feels like? So, I drank something, and it went away, I was like, oh…OH!

Huge aha moment!

That's when I started to realize, I had a brand new system that I had to get to know as if I were a newborn, as a matter of fact, with the surgery that I had, you have a timeline of your food type intake and after the day of your surgery, you have 21 days to re-introduce yourself back to solid food. Meaning, for me I was given a chart that was broken up by phases in which I was instructed on what I could consume from each food group for a certain number of days. My plan was separated into Phase One: Days 1-14, Phase Two: Days 15-28, and the Final Phase: Days 29-56. I wasn't allowed to eat solid soft meats or veggies and some wheat until day 29. Things like rice, pasta, alcohol, and raw veggies, were after 6 months.

That's a long ass time. Not the first week, because I was just coming out of surgery and I really didn't want to eat anything anyway, but by the end of that first week, you're looking at all the food in your kitchen and at commercials like a fiend. I was craving foods that I had never craved before. I remember just wanting a banana, an orange, or even a carrot.

I was craving stuff that I hadn't craved for years, and I just started to miss solid food. I just wanted to eat something solid, and I was thinking that this was so weird and if I was that weak. I began to research and discovered on the forums that I wasn't the only one as this happens with almost everybody, however, some people succumbed to the cravings, which can shorten the "honeymoon phase" of your weight loss period. The honeymoon phase is the length of time your body takes to lose weight and reset itself to a new factory default. Because I had the DS surgery, my average phase was going to be about 1 ½ years so I had that amount of time to capitalize on rapid weight loss before my body plateaued and reached its new default.

Here comes the great news!

I was losing weight like never before. It almost seemed unreal because at first, when I started weighing myself, I saw the scale move two pounds which was cool. The next day, nothing, but day three, four pounds dropped! I couldn't believe it... Four pounds in just one day!?!?!

This is not real.

I started checking the scale to see if it was off, maybe I'd broken it before the surgery, and I needed to buy another scale. Then, day four and five were two pounds each, day seven four more pounds, then the next day three more pounds. Every day it seemed like I was dropping weight. I was like, this is cra-mazing. Yes, crazy, and amazing... New word!! At that time, I wasn't even exercising, I was just walking, thanks to Adriane, who would pick me up just to make sure I was following the doctor's advice to stay active and avoid blood clots by walking regularly.

All that weight loss encouraged me to stick to the eating plan even more.

It was recommended that I have Pepcid AC on hand if I had any bouts of acid reflux which was common. I also had to begin taking my bariatric multivitamin, but for some reason, I couldn't keep it down so they had to prescribe me the liquid version until my body would accept the pill form. I can't stress enough how important it was that I paid attention to my new body and how it worked. Since I had both a restrictive and malabsorptive procedure, I had to pay close attention to how much I was eating and what I was eating because, during this period of trial and error, I vomited frequently. My body changed constantly, some foods that were fine to eat one day would come back up the next day, even if they were the same foods and portions.

Overeating was a no-no. To this day, I can eat a meal, or a snack and I will look down and just know that the last spoon or forkful I ate should be the last. The next one will drive me over the edge, and I will vomit. Believe me, I have tested it several times because the food was so good, but I paid severely for it. So, for a few weeks, I was getting to know the rhythm of my body's food and liquid intake.

This is where I began to have complications.

About three weeks after the surgery, I was starting to get the hang of how my new tool works (this is what they call your new body system...the Tool), but all of a sudden, I couldn't eat that much. I started vomiting more and more, but I attributed it to growing pains. Then I started to eat less and less, and this started on a Tuesday so by Friday, I was just back to drinking broth again, and then I didn't wanna do that because that started coming up. The liquid vitamins they prescribed because I couldn't keep down the pills also started coming back up. I was still convinced that this was part of the process so calling my surgeon was unnecessary. I started to feel back pain and stomach pain. But I was convinced it was pains from my body still healing from the surgery. By Saturday, I didn't think I had hardly anything to eat or drink. Sunday, I had coveted floor seat tickets to the Lemonade concert, which I had bought months in advance, so I was super excited to attend. I didn't care if I had to limp to this concert I was going and everyone I knew declined to buy a ticket with me, so I was going solo. In retrospect, not a wise move at all.

TRANSFORMED

Sunday morning arrived and I was not feeling well. I was a little weak, but I still attested to getting used to my new normal. I'm not eating as much so of course I'm a little bit sluggish. I remember as I was walking out the door, my brother asked, "So you're going?" I told him yes, but I didn't feel too good. He responded, "Then don't go." I thought to myself, "Bullshit" and headed toward the train station to the arena.

I got to the concert, and one positive aspect of that night was that I was still around 340 pounds, but I wanted to buy a T-shirt to commemorate the occasion. Of course, there weren't any 3x sizes, but something inside said to get a large size because you are going to wear that size soon. I purchased water as well and waited for the concert to begin. I took three sips and knew I couldn't take another sip, or everything would come back up.

The show began and I was on my feet like everybody else trying to enjoy the experience. A quarter of the way through the concert... I literally, for the first time in my life, had to sit down and watch through the screen. I got up occasionally just to look but I was getting weaker and weaker by the minute, and I started to break out in a cold sweat. Again, I was attesting this to maybe it's just too hot in here or I am moving too much, and I just had surgery a few weeks ago, so let me just calm down. By the time the concert was over, I got up and I was praying to God/Goddess to just let me make it back to where I parked my car as took the train downtown.

So, I'm just walking through the crowds, trying not to think about the journey, just putting one foot in front of the other and focusing. I got on the train, got to my car, and drove home pretty much on autopilot. When I arrived home, I allowed myself to feel that exhaustion. I was too weak to take a shower that night, I literally collapsed on the bed. The next day, outside of showering, I didn't move from my recliner chair in my room.

I got a call at about 5 o'clock, which was a daily check-in from my sis Adriane, and she asked how it was. I told her the concert was great! She said and I quote, " Stupid, I'm not talking about a concert, I'm talking about how you did out there by yourself?" I paused and something said to tell the truth. I told her, " I don't feel good."

She asked what was wrong and I told her everything that had happened since Tuesday. I didn't realize that I hadn't used the restroom all day on Sunday. The last time I think I used the restroom was Saturday and It is now Monday evening. She told me to call the doctor because something was wrong, and I should call her back right after. Now, I already know what that means.

She didn't believe I was gonna call the doctor, so that's her way of making sure that I called, so I hung up and called my doctor's office.

I talked to his assistant and told her the symptoms: stomach pain, back pain, severe nausea, and I couldn't keep anything down, not even water. She told me he was on vacation, but his partner could attend to me. She said she would reach out to his partner and call me back with instructions. I proceeded to call and tell Adriane what was going on when my call waiting went off with a private number. I answered and it was my surgeon who called me directly, while on vacation! This man is one of the good ones, no, he is one of the great ones to take time out of his vacation to find out what was going on with me, while having a perfectly capable doctor on call. I relayed the symptoms, and he advised me to go to the emergency room to get checked out and then they would call his team with the report. I called Adriane back letting her know I was going to the Emergency Room, and she asked if I wanted her to come get me, but I declined. I was thinking they would just give me some fluids to get me up to speed and I should be good to go.

Mamma used to say, "That's what you get for thinking." This was one of those times.

I dressed and drove myself to the hospital. I was really weak by this time, and I got called to the back almost immediately. I told them my symptoms, they took my pulse, and the nurse gave me a strange look. She told me they needed me to give a urine sample and I told them I hadn't been able to urinate for almost 48 hours. They sat me in the waiting area for about 15 minutes then I was called back, and by this time I felt like I was about to collapse if I didn't lay down somewhere soon. They walked me past the triage area for emergency people and my spidey sense started going off. I don't know about this. I was escorted into this room, and they proceeded to try to get me on an IV, but it was not working. The attendant keeps looking at my arms, hands, and feet over and over like something is going to mysteriously appear.

She told me she would be right back. A few minutes later, she reappeared with a friend and explained she was a vein specialist, because they couldn't access my veins as I was too dehydrated, and they were going to try another method which is putting the IV in my breast. I had never heard of such a thing in my life. Were they seriously going to put a needle in my breast!?! Absolutely.

As soon as the first couple of drips entered my bloodstream, I started dry heaving then vomited bile and the pain was so great I was shaking at this point. An older nurse walked in, and I truly love my older women of color because they're so mothering regardless of who you are or your age. She provided me with alcohol wipes to put on my nose to help with the nausea. Then she told me she was going to give me something for the nausea in my IV and it would taste funny at first, but it'll calm me down. Once she did that, she began preparing for me to be transported to get an MRI scan. She asked if

I had weight loss surgery and I told her I did and now I regretted doing it because I was in so much pain.

As she was rolling me to get the X-rays, she said, "I get it, you're in pain right now, and I feel you. But I promise you, mark my words. This is gonna pass and in a year's time, you're gonna know for a fact that this was the best decision that you ever made, and whatever pain you are going through now was worth it."

No truer words were spoken and again I thank Source for sending me what I needed when I needed it.

We completed the tests, and she took me back to my room. A few minutes later, another doctor entered the room and by then, I was feeling better as the meds had kicked in. Not only did they give me nausea medication, but they also administered something for the pain, so I was feeling better than I had in days. I perked up ready to hear the spiel that this was part of the process and that once the IV was completed I could roll out.

Umm...

He proceeds to tell me that he spoke with my surgeon's partner who is on call, and they decided to admit me, and yada, yada, yada. I say yada, yada, yada because, for a split second or three, I couldn't make out anything he was saying because I was stuck on the 'admitting me' part.

I had to tell him to start again, and he was very chipper as he was letting me know that they were keeping me because I had pancreatitis. He proceeded to tell me that the nurse would be in to relocate me to a holding room until my room upstairs was ready. He ended the speech with a smile and an emphatic, "You'll be fine."

I didn't even know what pancreatitis was, but I knew the pancreas was important, so now, I, for the first time, was scared. It was at that point I snapped back to reality and started asking questions like, "What exactly is Pancreatitis?" He explained that it was when your pancreas was inflamed or infected. A lot of times you contract it from alcoholism but there are times, like in this case when it happens from abdominal surgery.

I had to call everyone and let them know what was going on and that I was not returning home as planned. My Mom was freaking out and regretted returning to Florida so soon after my surgery. My friends were asking if they should come up because I was completely alone. But this was a school night and they had children, so I told everyone that... I'll be fine.

My friend Michelle, who was one of my treadmill walker buddies, came because she lived up the street from the hospital and pretty much didn't take no for an answer which made everyone feel a lot better that I wasn't alone. Michelle stayed with me until about midnight when they transported me to the other waiting room. I was finally able to get a few hours of restful sleep and then the orderly arrived to move me to my new room upstairs around 5 am.

It was now Tuesday, and I still hadn't used the restroom, I had two jumbo double bags of fluid pumped into me from the time I arrived until now. When the nurse asked if I could urinate because they needed a sample, this was the first time that I felt that I might be able to comply with the request. When you're in that situation, they want to measure your urine, so you're relieving yourself in this little measuring bucket inside the toilet.

I remember using the restroom and rejoicing but it literally was like very, very little, maybe an ounce at best and it was completely brown. I thought, " Lord, I'm dying. There is no such thing as brown urine!" The nurses proceeded to get me settled in and they were so very nice. Not one of them let on how serious this was.

The doctor came a couple of hours later as he does surgeries on Tuesday, and he stopped by to see how I was doing. That's when he told me I was staying for a few days and I was on a no-eat, no-drink diet. Everything that I would eat, and drink would be given intravenously. So, I had a white bag for hydration and a yellow bag for my food. Then I will be reintroduced to food in a couple of days.

In my mind, all I heard was I was not leaving this place for a minute. This is now the second time in one year that I'm in the hospital. I hardly go to the hospital, and now I'm in here twice in one year but this time I have no idea when I'm leaving. I don't think at this point in my life, outside of my car accident when I was two, that I have ever been in the hospital for a long period of time. No period, actually. I would go to the hospital, get treated, and come right back the same day.

Now, the fun part about hospitals is you're supposed to get this rest, but everybody's on a different schedule, and I wish they would come together and have a group meeting, so if the people that come to take your vitals, the group that takes your blood, the people that give you meds and the person that comes to walk you, could all get on one accord that would be great. Go get walked, take my blood, take my vitals, and give me my medicine all at the same time thus allowing me to sleep for more than two hours at a time day or night would be awesome.

I was hospitalized for a little under a week, and Thursday was when they first started to introduce food back into my diet. I had to undergo a series of tests during all of this and bless her heart, the young lady who came to wheel me to one of my tests. She was the one who spilled the tea on how serious my situation was. She proceeded to tell me she saw the chart and the severity of my illness when I arrived, and some people have died from being that far along.

Wait, WTF!?! Did she really just tell me that?

Clearly, the medical staff didn't want to divulge that type of information because they didn't want to tell somebody in the hospital that they could die from an illness. They try to keep your spirits up because the mind is a powerful thing. You are telling someone they might expire could actually cause them to give up.

PSA: Note to all the people in the medical field, if you're one of those little wonderful people who transport people back and forth for tests, don't divulge such information, because I know you are just making conversation, but you can adversely affect the outcome for some patients.

Now that I realized how serious it was, I was panicking and started to ask any and every one of my nurses if I was okay. But my caregivers, including my surgeon, who came for regular visits, had all assured me my vitals are great, I am hydrating nicely, and everything is... Fine. But my head was on a swivel, and I started watching everyone's expressions when they read the charts or came in for checkups.

At this point, I can feel myself kind of swelling up a little bit. One day, I happened to look down at my gargantuan breasts and realized that the breast that had the IV in it, the nipple was inverted. Ummm, this was definitely not how it was when I came here. I let the nurse know and showed her what I was talking about. She responds with, "Oh." Now, the way she said this "Oh" meant, "Oh shit, I ain't never seen anything like this and I need to get someone."

Another piece of advice... keep the poker face folks because we don't know if something is weird or that this is something you've never seen before. So, put a smile on your face and tell us, you will be right back and fall apart when you leave the room. Now I'm thinking, "Oh shit, I'm about to lose my boob." She returned with friends and by that time, there was a pool of cold liquid in my breast because the vein in my breast had blown. They advised I should be hydrated enough to move it to my arm, which they did successfully. By the next day, that one blew as well.

Dammit!

The reason my veins were blowing so quickly was there was so much fluid coming into my body because I needed to stay hydrated, and I also needed to be fed. At this point, they had to get this machine called the vein finder to locate another viable vein in my body where I could hold an IV. They removed the jumbo fluid bags, and I was given a regular-sized bag. I was also introduced to solid food, but I was still getting the nutrients in the yellow bag because they can't rely on what I am able to take in just yet. By the weekend, I was keeping all food, liquid, and meds down orally, so I was free to be discharged.

All was right with the world.

I got home and immediately got on that damn scale. I had gained 23 pounds in one week. I thought I was going to kill myself. I thought that somehow the procedure was reversed in the hospital or all the weight I had lost was just due to pancreatitis, and now that I was healed, the weight was back. But it was really all the fluid they had pumped into me. Needless to say, the surgery wasn't miraculously reversed and after about a week, I dropped that weight. However, this caused me to hawk that scale on almost a daily basis for years.

That ordeal was the only medical complication that I had resulting from the surgery. I have heard other horror stories, so with those stories compared to what I went through, I'll take mine. But understand not everyone has a horror story. Some people have zero complications so don't let anyone's experience stop you from pursuing what you want.

Now, as far as the day-to-day, your body goes through a series of adjustments. You just had major life-altering surgery, so you must adjust to a whole new you many times over. At first, I couldn't have a fan or the AC blowing directly in my face because for some reason it seemed like the air filled up my new stomach and made me nauseous. That was fun, especially when summer hit. I could not eat and talk because too much air was getting into my body when I talked, and since I only had a small space to put the food, the food and the air were battling with one another, which made me full quicker and made me nauseous. I was advised not to eat and drink at the same time. This is very important people, so I'm gonna say it once more time for the people in the back:

You cannot eat and drink at the same time.

I could drink right up until the moment I took my first bite, then once I took my last bite, that's when you start the clock for the 30-minute waiting period to drink something. So, I hope you don't eat anything that will make you extra thirsty, or something spicy because you can't drink for 30 minutes. Why? Because number one, you might throw up as there's nowhere for that fluid to go because you have filled up the little pocket. Number two, you might stretch out the little pocket.

PSA: Never trust a fart.

Also, in the beginning, I'm gonna be completely transparent in this book and give it to you raw because I want people to be prepared for some things I was not prepared for, and I had to look it up, because even the doctor didn't tell me that this might happen…there may be oil slicks. The surgery I had was mal-absorptive and restrictive, but mal-absorptive is the focal point for this piece of information, so my body does not absorb oil the way most people do because I'm not absorbing all the food. If I'm taking too much oil, it will come back out. Now, in the very beginning, in the first year of the surgery, when I began to eat stuff that had more oil in it, it didn't wait to come out, therefore when I went to the bathroom, it literally had seeped out in my underwear. Plus, there were times when I passed gas I would get an oil slick, which is an orangey putrid situation to have to deal with if you are in public.

I think the only people that don't have the problem, maybe with the poop or the gas, are people with the sleeve because they're intestines are not re-routed. The only thing that happens to them is that their stomach is cut down to the size of a banana. Lucky ducks.

Fun fact: Just because you had a weight loss surgery does not mean that you can't gain your weight back and then some. The stomach is a muscle, it expands, it contracts, and you can stretch that damn thing right back out and begin to overeat.

It'll take you a little longer than your regular stomach, but it can be done, and it has been done. I'm noticing a lot of people walking around here that look like they've never had surgery and are obese or morbidly obese because they stretched their stomachs out. Treat this like the tool it's supposed to be and don't abuse it. Every doctor will give you a guideline, follow their timeline and food guidelines. Go by the instructions and don't try to cut corners because it's not going to benefit you in the long run. The reason why I am maintaining my goal weight today is because I did not cut corners in the beginning, I was strict with it, I followed it by the book, and I made sure I adhered to all of my doctor's instructions.

Yes, I wanted some bread. Yes, I wanted some rice. Yes, I want some pasta. Yes, I wanted some fried chicken, and hell Yes, I wanted a soda, but I couldn't have those things (not yet). I made the decision to have this WLS and I was going to stick to it by any means necessary, I only had a certain window as far as the optimal period of weight loss, and I wanted to make sure that I utilized that time wisely.

PSA: Soda or any carbonation is not your friend. For those who have the DS or gastric surgery, the pain and bloating will be immense and so will the gas. For everyone, carbonated gas will start to stretch your stomach which will allow you to eat more than you should which can cause weight gain.

So, I want to put that bug in your ear. I still went through the surgery thinking in my head, that I was never gonna have carbonation again in life, and that's how committed I was, but as time went on, I started to learn my body. I started to be mindful of how much I was eating, what I was eating, what put weight on me, and what seemed to have no effect on my body.

What is the Blueprint?

I've had so many people ask me what my eating regimen was and that includes people who have had the surgery as well as those that didn't. My answer is always the same, I can't tell you what the blueprint is, I can only tell you what worked for me. I can tell you to stick to the general rules that I just laid out and that your doctor or nutritionist provides and really pay attention to your body. I can tell you, just like everyone else, there is a hierarchy to the food chain: protein, veggies, then starches and grains. This is common nutritional knowledge, and it still applies to those who have undergone surgery.

The little egg-sized stomach, if you have the DS or gastric bypass, or the banana if you have the sleeve is all you are working with, so you must make a choice: do I eat to live or live to eat?

Bottom line: you must change the way you think about and take in your food.

Let's talk about water.

Water, water, water, and then more water. I don't like drinking water like that, but you must drink water like that, so I keep cute little water bottles to track how much water I am consuming. I am horrible at measuring it but if I drink the full bottle, I know I am doing okay.

Hydration is key, and not juices, but actual water. Now, do I drink enough water right now? Mind ya business... But in the beginning, drink that damn water, and make sure you eat your food in the proper rotation so that you get all your nutrients because you're going to need it and you'll see the results.

I was dropping weight like nobody's business, by the time I went on my trip to Jamaica in November of 2016, remember I had my surgery in April of the same year, I was just under 300 pounds. So, I was shedding rapidly but again, I maintained the proper dietary requirements that I was supposed to, which is key. I think I dropped another 30 pounds by the time I celebrated New Year 2017. That's how fast it was coming off.

By the time I hit my 1st year surgiversary, I had hit the 250-pound mark.

Remember, this journey is yours and you are responsible for a lot of the work. Unless you have money for a steady nutritionist to design your meal plan, a personal trainer, and a chef to prepare your meals, you are doing all of this on your own. I encourage you to choose a support system and choose wisely. Try to assemble a squad that will encourage you and are into some of the same things to achieve your goal. If there is no one in your circle, go find your tribe, be it support groups that some of the bariatric programs facilitate or join a social media group.

I was fortunate to have had people in my life who were already into fitness, and into eating clean, so if I had questions, I was able to ask them, and they were there to support me and guide me. Since this was already a part of their lifestyle, it wasn't like they were changing their habits for me, I was actually getting more on board with them, which was so helpful.

And they were quite pleased, the lashing out stopped!

But seriously, you must have a good support system. I have heard stories where the only person in the house or in the friend group had surgery and everyone else was not only continuing to eat the way they used to eat but they also encouraged the person to fall off the wagon or berated them for trying to lose weight. I'm not saying that everyone in your life is going to be on board, some people will continue the path that is for them. What I am saying is that if you are one of those people who chooses to stay where you are, you can still encourage others who are choosing to make a change.

PSA: Not everyone is destined to go where you are going and that's okay.

I have a friend who is also overweight and did not change her habits, however, she didn't knock what I was doing, and she was very supportive of the change I was making. Did that inspire her to make a change? No. Will she ever make that change? I don't know, but I support her in whatever decision she makes for her journey, and I will be there for her either way.

And I have another friend who was like, "But I thought we were eating buddies so what are we gonna do now?" I replied, "Find something else to damn do because I can't do that anymore. So, either we find something else to do and we don't bond over food, or I just don't see you until I get my shit under control." We wound up taking a break and only talked over the phone. Then he started to take his health and weight seriously, so now he understands, and we hang out often.

There was another friend who did not want me to have the surgery. She felt like I should do it naturally and didn't support my decision. Once I had the surgery and the weight started coming off, she became more hostile and bitter. She is no longer in my life.

If you have people like that and they really don't want to support you, either they shut up or get out, those are the only two options, because they shouldn't be allowed to bring that toxicity into your life, and I would give that advice to anybody.

You can't control other people, but you can control who is around you and how they are going to contribute to your journey. This is not only for weight loss but also for any area in your life that you would like to see transformed into what you desire.

Let no one stop you from being the best version of you.

CHAPTER 7

The One-der Years

I am now entering the mystical land of one-der.

By the time the Summer of 2017 rolled around I had dropped so much weight, I was unrecognizable by some of my friends who hadn't seen my day-to-day transformation. I was still sticking to a solid eating plan and remaining active through walking. I recall the day "it" happened, I stepped on the scale and BOOM it read 199! I had reached the promised land, one-derland as some people affectionately call it. This is when you reach a number that begins with a 1, which I hadn't seen in decades. I wanted to commemorate the occasion by doing something that I hadn't done before as I didn't want to go have a meal…too cliche. I chose to invite all my friends to attend a belly dance class with me and it was glorious. I was on cloud nine and felt amazing that I was starting to venture out to do things that I wouldn't have done because of my size.

Now, when you lose as much weight as I did, which by then I had lost over 170 pounds, they warn you, there are a couple of things that could possibly happen, one is long-term, and one is short-term. The long-term one is some people after a couple of years would lose their teeth. That hasn't happened to me. The short term is because you're losing weight so rapidly and you're not getting the proper nutrients that your body needs, the body is very smart and it will compensate by dropping things it feels like it doesn't need to nourish, your hair being one of them.

Never say what you will never do!

I was happy I was forewarned because I did lose my hair. My hair shed so badly, that it was equivalent to a person going through chemo, it was literally shedding almost daily. It was getting so thin and wispy, that people who knew me knew I was like Samson from the bible, my crowning glory was my hair. I loved it. So, losing my hair was like a sacrifice to the weight loss gods, and I remember having to sit in the salon chair and make the decision to do a big chop because it was just too thin at that point. It wasn't breaking off; it was literally falling out from the root.

I wound up having to cut most of my hair down to the scalp, and my hair stylist at the time left enough of a tuft at the top of my head to cover a track, and she just weaved in a bob with blond highlights.

This turned into a whole blonde era, which is crazy because I was adamant that I would never wear blonde hair, would never cut my hair, and would never go natural. Up until that point, I had relaxed hair all my adult life but when I got the big chop, I just decided not to have any relaxers anymore, so whatever hair was gonna grow after that, it was going to be au natural.

Prepare for the new normal...whatever that may be.

I was a pretty regular person bathroom-wise before the surgery, so I was expecting that to not change. Now the window is shorter from the time that I eat to the time I have to go to the bathroom. I may have eaten breakfast and lunch before, and I wouldn't have to go to the bathroom until I got home from work, or if I ate a big meal the evening before and then the next morning here it comes. Now, I must do it in the morning like clockwork, there's no way of getting around that, no matter if I eat early, late, or not at all. Also, if I eat breakfast or if I don't eat breakfast, in the afternoon I was going to go to the bathroom again. If I eat for sure, I will be going to the bathroom within the four-hour period to get that out, it does not stay because we don't absorb everything, so it's almost like a one-way express ticket out. So, you have to plan accordingly. Don't get caught out there, because, at the same time, when you have to go, you have a very short window of when you get that feeling, you

TRANSFORMED

better high tail it to the toilet because you ain't gonna be able to hold it.

That proves to be problematic sometimes if you're traveling or if you're gonna be out all day. I have to plan my eating around what I'm doing that day, and if I'm gonna be able to get to a comfortable bathroom. I realized this when I had to take a trip overseas for the first time, post-surgery, I was about 165 pounds, and I was going to be overseas for about three weeks. The travel time, because I was going to Morocco and traveling as cheaply as I could, was a long trip. I took three flights with layovers to get there, and I tried to plan it so that I wouldn't be stuck on a plane and have to poop. Let me tell you something, that smell is horrible! The medical staff didn't prepare me for that, and I was trying to figure out why, so of course I looked it up because I always like to do research to see if I'm an anomaly, which I wasn't. The reason why it smells so bad is because we don't digest and break down the food all the way, so when it bypasses some of the intestines, it's sitting in your bowels smelling like the equivalent of rotting food that's sitting outside in 100-degree weather.

The plane rides were okay, and I wound up landing in Portugal for the second layover, so I was able to handle my business, but I was still thrown off just simply because of traveling to a strange place and the time zone difference caused a glitch in the matrix but all was well once I settled in Morocco.

When I was in Morocco, we were doing a traveling Caravan for about 4-5 days, and because I wasn't always near a bathroom or it wasn't a restroom I was accustomed to using, it started to affect my stomach and I became bloated. I wound up having to hold it, throwing my entire body clock off which made me a little ill. I made the decision, which I do not recommend, I'm saying it again, **I do not recommend this**, to eat less, so I would use the bathroom less, therefore eliminating the problem. I lost quite a bit of weight when I was in Africa, and by the time I arrived in Paris to visit for a few days with a friend, it was very noticeable. As soon as he saw me, he was like, "What the hell happened to you in Africa? Why are you so skinny? We need to go eat right now." I felt that I had lost some weight on that trip, but I really knew it when he was staring at me like he was about to sponsor me for 39 cents a day.

This may not be the case for everyone and as time has passed, my tolerance has gotten better and I instinctively know when, what, and how much to consume to move accordingly. Again, I say, you must pay attention to your new body and what works for you.

Peeling back the onion.

TRANSFORMED

While I was losing weight, I was still attending my therapy sessions faithfully. I'm so glad that I did because it seemed that as I was coming down on the scale, any major issues I had when I was that weight was bubbling up to the surface. For example, when I arrived at around the low 300's, I dealt with my daddy issues.

Storytime:

As I stated before, I am no stranger to spiritual gifts, as I have my own. One of which is Oneiromancy, which basically is prophetic dreams (you know I had to get both fancy and technical on ya!) I also communicate with people on the other side, especially the Ancestral realm. I have had dreams about my ancestors, some of whom I had never met in this life as they transitioned before my birth.

While I was unpacking my daddy issues, I began to have dreams about him. In the first dream, I saw him standing at my window, and he was trying to get into the house. I politely told him he was dead, and I wasn't interested in dying too. See the old folks used to say if a dead person comes to you and you go with them you die. I wasn't giving him the opportunity to approach me at all. It was Mamma who advised me to see what he wanted as it seemed like he wanted to tell me something. I guess he figured he would take another approach because the next dream I had, he sent for me. Every dream

TRANSFORMED

I have about the other side I travel there by some mode of transportation, plane, car, or train. I think this is their way of not freaking me out and letting me know that I am safe and have the means to get back.

When I arrived, my dad and I, along with my brother and sister, did things that I always wanted to do with him. We went to amusement parks, played games, and went to sporting events. After we were done, I awakened. It was as if he was giving me the childhood I always wanted. The final dream came, and we pretty much did the same thing, except this time he dropped me off at a train station and told me to go with his brother, who is still living, to buy tickets. Something felt very final about this time, so I refused. My uncle came and got me and stated we would buy the tickets and come right back, I agreed and went with him. I turned and looked back, and my handsome young father was smiling next to his car and waving. Somehow, we bought the tickets on the train and when I went to go back, my uncle stated I couldn't, and the train left. That was the last time he came to me. Later, I would have a reiki session with a shaman, and he would reveal to me that my dad made peace with everyone and that he chose to return to The Light.

But every so often, when I think about him or when I feel like I need my dad, that Petey Pablo song "Raise Up" will play (which I found out years later he loved that song (Ol' North Carolina man he was) to remind me that he is always nearby.

This peeling back the onion of weight and emotions occurred during the entire time I was losing weight. I finally dealt with and confronted people who I had issues with and was able to let a few friendships go while renewing and strengthening others. The hardest issues were the sexual assaults that I carried. A few years before I lost weight, my ex-boyfriend from the first adult assault reached out to me and apologized for what happened and how he treated me. I forgave him then, but I really didn't process it until therapy. But now, I have made peace with myself, and forgiven him for what happened.

Plus, I started to have a real connection to God/Goddess and after that life-changing dream, I embarked on a spiritual journey. I delved into meditation and started to peel back the layers of all the religions I had experienced as well as the ones it seemed my ancestors practiced trying to find what resonated with my soul.

It's so funny because therapy played a major role in leading me back on a spiritual path.

Another thing I wasn't prepared for was how expensive it was to change my wardrobe as I was coming down from a 400-pound body. I was and still am a fashionista, so my walk-in closet, side closet, and downstairs coat closet were full of clothes. I had jewelry, rings, bangles, watches, anklets, toe rings, chokers, hats, hats, and more hats. She, me, her, loves to shop!

Now, in the beginning, I didn't have to shop because things were loose, but they were workable. Once I went from a size 30-32 to a size 24, I couldn't wear the 30-32's I had in my closet. So, I had to get rid of those. Then the 26-28 sizes started looking really loose, and I'm talking about everything, bras, your undies and shapewear, your socks, even your shoes, slippers, and flip-flops! Everything in your wardrobe you lose. Also, I think I lost half an inch of my height. I was 5 '5 ½ pre-surgery and now I'm 5' 5 even, so I lost half an inch. How is that even possible you ask? Because people don't understand when you are as big as I was, my feet are fat and that raises you up a little bit. I had fat in my joints, whether it's your knee joints, or your hip joints, that raises you up a little bit. I even had fat in my head because I noticed that when I lost weight, I didn't wear the same hat size anymore. My head shrunk, my hands and feet shrunk. Because my feet were so fat, I could wear either a size 9 1/2 wide or 10 wide. I now wear between an 8-9 regular, based on the cut of the shoe. Mind you, I had to get rid of over 75 pairs of shoes, not counting sneakers, boots, sandals, etc.

When I first started to have to get rid of clothes it made me nervous. I had not seen a size 24, let alone a size 20 in years and I was so very terrified that if I got rid of the sizes, somehow, I would have to buy them back if I gained weight again. What I did was, I got to the point where people would say, "Hey buddy, you look crazy in these gargantuan clothes," and that's what I knew, I had to go ahead and replace my old sizes with new ones. Some clothes were so cute or sassy that I felt I didn't want to part with them so I thought maybe I could tailor them. Let me tell you, by the time you go get a tailor, you will have to pay more money than if you just bought something else equivalent to that item in the new size. I resized a few select items that I really couldn't find, and I paid a pretty penny to do it. For a while, I stopped buying any kind of jewelry. The only accessories I still had were some necklaces, earrings, and scarves. That was about it.

Getting rid of my wardrobe was a big deal because that signified that that old life was gone, and I was making the commitment that I wasn't going back thus throwing away the safety net and literally putting my money where my mouth was. So, I got rid of all my bras and underwear, my socks, my rings, my bangles because they just fell off my hand when I put my arm down, anklets, toe rings, and all my footwear. Some I donated to thrift stores, and some I gave to friends that were still that size, which I subsequently did each time I dropped significantly. I didn't replace my entire wardrobe, every dress size as that would have bankrupted me!

TRANSFORMED

I don't think I was truly ready for this part. Not just financially but emotionally as well. In my case, my entire wardrobe, which is a part of me, not just physically, but it's a part of me emotionally, as I hand-picked these clothes, and created these ensembles to look and feel a certain way, but now all of that is gone. It's like I was wiping the slate clean and starting from scratch. I remember when I packed my final haul to take to the thrift store, I cried.

Like I stated before, on top of being emotional, it's expensive. That's why I will suggest to everyone, maybe put, if you can, a little money away for your wardrobe as you tick down in size. I literally lived at thrift stores and clearance racks, and I waited until the things were just way too damn big before I dropped to the next size and bought as little as I could, concentrating on stretch pants because they were cheap. On top of that, some people were giving me clothes that were the size that I was in, so that was a huge blessing.

PSA: Don't be too proud or too ashamed to take some hand-me-downs as that will save your life and save your pockets, because trust me, you're gonna need the money later on down the line to restock your actual wardrobe.

I can tell you that I do not own, except for two of my watches and a shirt because they're little keepsakes plus a pair of jeans that you see on the back cover, a single solitary piece of clothing or jewelry from that time outside of t-shirts I wear around the house. I had to get rid of everything.

Somehow you never see it coming until it's here.

Remember when I said therapy led me back to my spiritual path? What I didn't know was that it was for a very good reason. My grandmother, Mamma as I have called her since I was two years old and I couldn't say grandma anymore because my mouth was wrecked, had moved down to Georgia to live with my brother and me. By this time, I had returned to school for Motion Pictures and Television as I had been out of the game for so long that I felt like I needed to start over by going for my bachelor's degree. My niece also came to live with us so she could finish her junior and senior year at the school she wanted to attend. Even though I was still struggling financially, things were looking up and I felt I was moving in the right direction.

Then, I started to get spiritually uncomfortable, like something was about to change. I believe God/Goddess was preparing me for the series of events that were about to occur. Normally, as I learned in both my spiritual and therapeutic walk, my emotional weight manifests into physical weight, but now that I'd had the surgery, I was in uncharted territory as to how my body would respond to trauma. The first thing was finances, my new job which was heading me in the direction that later I would need wasn't paying like my last position and I got into major debt. My credit score tanked so I couldn't refinance my house so was forced to sell it to get out of debt. That was my first home purchase, and I was so proud of the way I had it decorated. I grew to love that home over time, and it devastated me more than anyone knew to sell it. Around the time this was happening, my uncle and godfather, died suddenly right before Thanksgiving 2017. That completely shook the family as he was the youngest of my grandmother's children. I was the one who had to break the news to my grandmother, and I swear she bucked like she had been shot. She was in complete disbelief. There had been close calls with some of her children, like my uncle who miraculously with one prosthetic leg made it down the steps of one of the twin tower buildings, but he survived. Then my mom had a near-fatal heart attack a couple of years prior, but she survived. No one saw this coming, and Mamma never recovered from that loss.

I sold my house at the beginning of 2018, and we moved to a rented house not too far from our old home. All that summer, a black butterfly came and sat on my porch. My grandmother turned 90 in June and the entire family came down to see her except for a cousin of mine who couldn't make it due to a summer school conflict with one of her daughters. Fall came and Mamma decided to visit that cousin. I remember this because the day she left, so did the black butterfly. While she was gone, I had a reiki session performed on me in the park and I had a vision of an eagle and then a vision I was holding my mom's hand as there was a death. Once I came out of the session, a black butterfly hit my head. I received a phone call the next morning at work from my brother who told me the news that Mamma had passed away and I collapsed. There are no words to express the pain of that loss. That woman came second only to my mother in this world. She was a constant in my life from the time I was born, so my brain couldn't comprehend a world where she was not.

Remember the Morocco trip I told you all about earlier, well that happened in 2019 almost a year after she passed away. When I began to prepare my wardrobe, I broke down crying because she knew about the trip but wasn't here in the physical. She was so very proud of me for losing weight and was held hostage to all the fashion shows I put on when I bought new clothes after reaching what I thought was my goal weight of 165 pounds. Before, when I called her or talked to her in Jersey, she would end the call with, "Don't forget to pray to lose weight." Now, she ends each conversation with, "Don't forget to pray for a husband." Plus, I could hear her talking to my mom on the phone every other day telling her how good I looked, but that I didn't need to lose any more weight and for her to be sure to tell me that!

Enter the baddest Ancestor of them all.

TRANSFORMED

Now Mamma was gone, and I didn't know how to move on. Immediately, she began to show up in my dreams. She knew I needed her to be with me so I could do what I needed to do for the rest of the family. She even came to me in a dream and told me to take the extended trip to Paris! I was planning the flights back as frugally as I could to return as fast as I could when she came to me and said she was moving out. I argued with her for a second trying to figure out why she was unhappy until it dawned on me, and I blurted out, "Mamma, you're dead!" She just looked at me sarcastically and I knew what she was saying. I wasn't tied to anyone anymore as my niece moved back in with her mom. I was free to start living life.

In October of 2018, I had to have fibroid surgery and my mom, of course, came up to care for me. I had another dream about Mamma and saw a green butterfly, so I knew she was watching over me.

Fun Fact: Mamma's favorite color is green (I say is… because she is still here). From that point of transition, I now see green butterflies when she is sending a wink. I love you, Lady.

Okay, let's take a couple of deep breaths and continue.

Sagging skin is a big factor and some people have a problem with the skin and will start to gain their weight back after seeing what they look like with the varying degrees of skin folds or sag. It's based on your body, where you lost, how big you were, and how much elasticity you did or did not have, which will denote how much excess skin you have. I lost weight all over pretty much evenly, so I had sagging skin all over.

I will have to get what they call a full body lift, and you can't get that all at one time, well not here in the states, they will not do it all at once. You must break it up because of health reasons. You can't have that much trauma to the body at one time. When I was big, like I had mentioned, I had had breasts for as long as I could remember. It seems like I had breasts since I was like two. I have a picture of me and the little baby bikini, and I filled out the top. It's crazy! So, I went from my highest cup size which was an I cup to I ain't got no breasts! Literally what people saw filling out my bra was skin. I took that bra off and these were some pancakes. And it's so weird because I went from having these huge natural breasts to having to get implants. When I went for a consultation, the doctor at the time told me that I was completely empty and that if I had the lift performed without implants, I would be completely flat. My first thought was, "I can't believe I gotta pay for titties!?!" The irony was not lost on me but ya gotta laugh at yourself!

I thought I was going to be the crusader to get the financial approval of the insurance companies because I believed it was medically necessary for me to have the skin surgery.

Absolutely Not.

There is still a battle waging between the doctors versus the insurance companies over the age-old question of, " Is skin removal surgery, either medically necessary or a cosmetic situation?" Right now, the insurance companies are very staunch in its position that that is a cosmetic choice. Personally I, as well as the therapist that I went to, and the PCP that I had, along with the plastic surgeons that I've talked to, as well as my bariatric team, all feel like skin surgery should be included because in a way you are still trapped in a body that you are not comfortable with, which takes a toll on your psyche to look at this new body, now looking like a sagging mess, which sometimes like I said, causes people to actually gain weight back in order to not look like that, because they don't want to see themselves that way.

It also affects your self-esteem because you still can't be free, you still must hide behind clothes, and also physically uncomfortable, especially while working out. You must make sure that your workout gear is on point because if you start running and jumping, that skin starts flapping, making noise, and pulling which hurts. I don't think that they understand that it's not just a cosmetic thing because one wants to look aesthetically pleasing, it's also because it will help mentally, emotionally, and physically so there's little chance of hurting yourself. But this was a battle that I did not win.

I went up against them three times. For the first petition to be deemed medically necessary, you must meet a certain criterion:

Number one, you must maintain your weight for, I believe, six months to a year post-surgery at a certain percentage of your former weight to be eligible.

Number two, you must have documentation over a long period of time that you have had sores and rashes and discoloration, possible growths and fungal smells documented by your doctor that they have tried to give you some type of medical salve or lotion or potion and it did not work. And that is another reason why you're a good candidate for the surgery.

Number three, As far as the stomach surgery, because 99 percent of the time they are only approving stomach skin removal, nothing else qualifies unless you really are having severe medical issues, but in order for you to just have the lower apron, which they call the lower stomach, the apron, to be removed, you also have to have it hanging a certain amount below your genitalia.

So, I had to jump through hoops to get the weight loss surgery and if you are successful at a significant amount of weight loss, I gotta double hoop and holler to maybe get a portion of my skin removed. Ridiculous.

Absolutely Not.

There is still a battle waging between the doctors versus the insurance companies over the age-old question of, " Is skin removal surgery, either medically necessary or a cosmetic situation?" Right now, the insurance companies are very staunch in its position that that is a cosmetic choice. Personally I, as well as the therapist that I went to, and the PCP that I had, along with the plastic surgeons that I've talked to, as well as my bariatric team, all feel like skin surgery should be included because in a way you are still trapped in a body that you are not comfortable with, which takes a toll on your psyche to look at this new body, now looking like a sagging mess, which sometimes like I said, causes people to actually gain weight back in order to not look like that, because they don't want to see themselves that way.

It also affects your self-esteem because you still can't be free, you still must hide behind clothes, and also physically uncomfortable, especially while working out. You must make sure that your workout gear is on point because if you start running and jumping, that skin starts flapping, making noise, and pulling which hurts. I don't think that they understand that it's not just a cosmetic thing because one wants to look aesthetically pleasing, it's also because it will help mentally, emotionally, and physically so there's little chance of hurting yourself. But this was a battle that I did not win.

I went up against them three times. For the first petition to be deemed medically necessary, you must meet a certain criterion:

Number one, you must maintain your weight for, I believe, six months to a year post-surgery at a certain percentage of your former weight to be eligible.

Number two, you must have documentation over a long period of time that you have had sores and rashes and discoloration, possible growths and fungal smells documented by your doctor that they have tried to give you some type of medical salve or lotion or potion and it did not work. And that is another reason why you're a good candidate for the surgery.

Number three, As far as the stomach surgery, because 99 percent of the time they are only approving stomach skin removal, nothing else qualifies unless you really are having severe medical issues, but in order for you to just have the lower apron, which they call the lower stomach, the apron, to be removed, you also have to have it hanging a certain amount below your genitalia.

So, I had to jump through hoops to get the weight loss surgery and if you are successful at a significant amount of weight loss, I gotta double hoop and holler to maybe get a portion of my skin removed. Ridiculous.

My apron didn't hang down past my vagina; it sort of hugged it and hung off to the sides. The rest of my body parts, I was on my own to pay for, but I thought if I could get them to do my stomach, that would be a good portion of the battle. I submitted my paperwork with a hopeful heart. I had a letter from the bariatric surgeon, a letter from my PCP, and a letter from plastic surgery with pictures and measurements. Everyone had the same recommendation.

They sent me back a letter with a polite hell no. Then I sent them back a letter to dispute and challenge the ruling, and they sent me back a letter stating that they said what they said.

I waited another year with another insurance company, this time my weight is holding between 145 and 149, so I'm in a really good position and a little more sag. I go to a different plastic surgeon, subject myself to standing stark naked under the brightest, most unforgiving lights as a stranger with an assistant watching, poked, and lifted your folds of flesh, mapping out what would be best to have done first.

When you lose weight, you lose weight everywhere.

For me, my first surgery would include removing the excess skin from my arms, stomach, and breasts as well as installing the implants. Having the insurance company cover the stomach portion would help financially for the hospital costs and it would also qualify you for a few weeks off for recovery as you would be eligible to take short-term disability.

Unfortunately, the first insurance company must have put my name out in these streets because the verdict from the second insurance company was a no and a polite, don't ask us anymore. I was on my own.

Now that I knew what I was up against, I started to plan for the multiple surgeries I would need. After the first round, they would like you to wait at least six to nine months between plastic surgeries. Phase two was going to be when I would have the excess skin removed from my thighs, my back, and my rear end with a lift. Both surgeries come with hospital fees and post-op treatments, ointments, and visits.

Then, to add insult to injury, I will need to have my face and neck lifted!

Normally I wouldn't have worried about a neck or face issue because black don't crack like that but understand black may not crack but when stretched black will sag. This new development has tacked on to a third phase of the surgery process that I didn't see coming. At the end of the day, the cost might run for a full body, face, and neck lift with breast implants anywhere from $50,000 to $70, 000 or higher in the states.

When you are losing weight, start pricing the costs of surgery and research the doctors in your area if you want to do it there or in a different part of the country where you live, or even if you want to have some of the procedures performed abroad. When choosing a doctor, hit the forums and see what their work looks like and if they are accustomed to working with your body type to give you the results you desire. A great thing to look out for is if they are well-versed in dealing with lifts or excess skin removal. Many plastic surgeons are great with the average tummy tuck or butt lift, but it takes certain surgeons to have the talent to remove large amounts of skin successfully if you are as large as I was and lost as much weight as I did. Plus, I made sure I researched doctors who were familiar with working with my shape, I am slender, but I have curves and I wanted to make sure that they didn't work with just boxy body types.

So that is my advice. Start doing your research on your doctor of choice and get your finances in order because it is expensive. Make sure you choose wisely and account for the time your body may need to heal and the time off work you will need to take to achieve optimal results.

CHAPTER 8
Friends, Men, And Dividends

The more you change, the more they say, "You changed."

How people treat the "new" you.

When I was bigger, people had a certain perception of me, "Oh, you're so wild and crazy, you have such a beautiful face and just a wonderful personality but will just say anything and get away with it!" Yeah, they were right, I was like that, and I'm still like that. At the same time, I was always invisible to men and cool with women, but then that started to change a little bit as I got smaller and smaller, and so now I'm more visible to men, and I am more judged and side-eyed by women.

Weirdly, people will sometimes judge you based on how they see themselves. As a big girl, when I would say things like, "I'm the bomb dot com." Or "Check me out, my outfit, hair, makeup…I'm doing the damn thing!!" I would get responses like, "Yeah, girl, you got that, you did that... Yeah, you look good girl!" If I say the same thing today, instead I will get, "You're stuck on yourself", or "You think you are too cute now, ever since you lost that weight, all of a sudden you are full of yourself." I said the same things when I was bigger, and I don't understand the difference. So, not only did I have to adjust how I viewed myself and come to grips that I was smaller and living in this new body, but I was also coming to grips that I was having new experiences with this new body as if I was a different person.

People think you're stuck on yourself or conceited if you have confidence in yourself, which leads me to believe that people like to give compliments if they feel like you or something about you is inferior. So, it's easy to tell the unattractive person that they are right and that they look good or got it going on because you feel like you are patting them on the head, or encouraging them to have confidence in themselves, but if you are attractive and say you know you look good all of a sudden, you're conceited. That's what some people do. Not everybody operates this way as some people are confident in themselves so it doesn't matter to them what size you are or what you look like, they will treat you the same. It's crazy to experience life on both sides of the fence.

Storytime!

I've also experienced just what is being said about big people when they are not around. One time, I was taking a flight via an airline where you gotta race for a damn seat because you don't get to pick your seat in advance. My group was up first, As I was boarding the plane, I saw there was a seat toward the front, like a whole row almost open, except for one white lady who was sitting on the aisle. As I was walking towards her, she was mean mugging me hard, so I thought she was one of those who don't like black people. But I don't really care because I'm sitting in front of this plane (thank you Rosa Parks). I paused and asked if these seats were taken and suddenly, her whole countenance changed and she said, "No, no, they're not taken... Come on in. They're totally available."

Huh? Okay, what the hell is going on with this white woman, seriously? I proceeded to sit down, and she said to me, "Oh my God, I'm so glad you sat here." Now at this point, I put a seat in between us, so I'm sitting in the window seat and she's sitting in the aisle because she was giving me straight-up 'Get Out' vibes. She continued to say, "I'm so glad that you sat here." and I said, "Really?" She responds, "Yeah, oh my God, I hate when I get stuck sitting with a fat person, now we only have to find another small person and then we're good." All I could say was, "Oh, okay?" I was in complete shock. I had no idea how to react to that because this woman didn't know my backstory. This person didn't know that she was talking to a former extreme morbid obese person, who is now hearing what people really are saying about fat people. Here I thought she was racist.

I didn't think people really said shit like that out loud to other people, they may have thought it, of course, but to really say it to another person, and a stranger on top of that like it was okay. She didn't know if I had an overweight significant other, children, or any other family member but still felt comfortable enough to say these things to me. She puts her bitch face back on, and low and behold a slim white lady comes down the aisle and asks cautiously if the seat was taken. She perked up again and responded the same way she did me. After we all got settled, she sat back and said, "Oh, I can relax now." And she looked quite pleased with herself. I was sitting there flabbergasted! This is a real fucking thing. People really do act like this... Seriously? These are conversations that strangers actually have about overweight people. Mind Blown.

Another time I can recall, I was at a very famous strip club here in Atlanta, very, very famous. And the place was jam-packed. Literally, every seat in the house was filled, so there were a lot of people standing up and they don't like patrons to stand anywhere near the aisles. Security marched up and down the aisles with their little flashlights yelling, "Clear the aisles, move to the side!" So, we were all standing to the side looking like we were waiting for government cheese handouts and I kind of moved over a little bit into the aisle; realizing what I did, I looked back nervously to the security guard who just finished yelling at some folks to get the hell out of the walkway. I moved over and apologized for getting too far over, but I couldn't see the stage.

He proceeded to signal at two ladies in front of me with his flashlight and said, "Oh no, you're good, you're good. I see why you had to move so you are good standing there. I know you can't see past these two biggums in the front, so you could stand right there because you are small enough, you're not gonna get it away." Mind you he just told these very women to get off the aisle. Again, people really do talk about big people behind their backs like that to strangers and are quite okay with it. He was also quite okay with being very nice to me and bent the rules for me, the small person, because of these "two biggums" in the front that to him, were clearly blocking my view. But I used to be that biggum, so he was talking about me and I'm thinking, clearly, this happens more often than not.

Experiences like this happened quite a few times, and the feeling I felt was almost equivalent to being a black person and being able to "pass" when you are now able to hear what white people say about black people when they are not in the room. Guilt started to set in as I felt like I was betraying my people because I didn't say anything.

What am I gonna say in the middle of a strip club, "You can't say that because I used to be fat too." I was like a deer caught in headlights. Even at work, some of the same folks that I was pretty much invisible and didn't really interact with suddenly spoke to me and addressed me by name and I didn't know they knew who I was. Now they are holding the doors and holding the elevators when I am a block away, whereas before they would let them close.

I've seen people make room for me and not make room for a bigger person. I've seen an overweight female standing, with men in the room, but then when I walked into the room, several men tried to offer me their seats and this transcended the color barrier as this was a white woman and a white man and the white man would offer his seat up for me.

Wow, this is really my new reality, the way people see me now was not the way that they saw me before, I'm being treated totally differently, and now transitioning to being a recipient of what they call "pretty privilege," and watching my former club get that treatment of either invisibility or unconscious bias. While some folks are downright mean-spirited and treat folks like crap because they can, I do believe some people have no idea that they are treating people a certain way or "sizing them up" based on their weight. Case in point, I noticed a few times, when I was in line to get food and a larger person was next to me, I watched the server give proportioned-sized servings to the bigger person and put extra on my plate. It's funny, I didn't notice it when I was the overweight person, but I'm paying closer attention now that I've had the opportunity to live two very different lives.

I began to defend my former club members, but I also noticed that women of a certain size began to treat me differently. I noticed that I would smile or be friendly to people of a certain size and they were either side eyeing me or looked like I was going to say something rude to them. Some colleagues that I had relationships with suddenly stopped speaking to me. I was having a conversation once with a colleague of mine about certain eating habits of overweight people and she happens to be plus-sized; she promptly told me I no longer had the right to have an opinion because I was not one of them anymore. She could talk all day, but I was officially out of the club. Apparently, the rule is one can talk trash about anyone openly if you are a member of the group, but no "outsiders" can do it. It's kind of like how People of color, LGBTQ+, or even your family can say things to and about each other, but if someone outside that circle says something out-of-pocket, it's on!

At this point I had to change some of the things I said because I wasn't fat anymore, so no, I can't talk about fat people and true confession, I didn't want to. I didn't wanna talk about fat people when I got smaller, the way I went in when I was plus-sized and believe me I went in on big people back then. A lot of it had to do with how I saw and felt about myself and seeing another big person was like looking into a mirror and seeing what I hated most. Nowadays, I have more compassion for my former club members than I ever did when I was a member. But I changed more than that. I was finding out who the real Nia was and what I wanted for the first time in my life.

PSA: Hey, listen, you may lose friends or the likes of co-workers when you find your true self. Who cares? Do not let these people push you back into the version of yourself that makes them comfortable. You were not put on this earth to make others comfortable; you were put here to live your life and learn your lessons. You live your life for YOU. No one gets a BOLO - buy one, live one free. Never let anyone dim your light. Shine Hunteys!!!! They will be okay as they will go with you on the ride or get off at the next stop... and if they do the latter, good riddance.

All those times I spent alone before, I didn't utilize that time to do this, so I now began my journey of self-discovery. My new spiritual foundation, which included meditation, reiki, and eventually a couple of shamanic-led cosmic journeys allowed me to understand further who I was to myself, my family, and the purpose I had for this lifetime. Plus, I was dating myself and getting to know and love all the little things that make up who I am. Making the decision to keep what served me and remove what didn't. I was never one to say I loved all of myself because I didn't. I also wasn't one of those beings who believed that you must love and accept yourself before you can make a change. To me, that was nonsense. I've noticed that what makes me change something about myself or where I am in life is a sense of discomfort. I don't like that part of me or the way this part looks or the job I was in, and that level of spiritual and physical discomfort propels me forward to make the change. For me, acceptance brings about complacency and when you are complacent you are hard-pressed to change your situation. Looking back on the major changes in my life, I was made to feel spiritual and physical unrest before the new transition occurred. Now I know how to recognize the feeling and I began to dig deep within to determine the next level I am about to embark on.

It's raining men! Well, maybe cloudy with a chance of drizzle...

I know you all have been waiting for this part...is she dating?

I was trying to date when I was in therapy, I was opening myself up to dating, so I joined dating sites and went on a couple of unsuccessful dates. I have used dating sites over the past few years, but I don't think the online thing is for me, but that is a preference on my part. Do men now notice me? Yes. Did they approach me? No. I'm thinking, well damn, now I'm small, like WTF? What is really going on with me? Am I still not attractive to men? I see them looking, I see them staring when I'm not looking, but they're not approaching me, like what's really going on? I realized that the energy I was projecting was off. But now, with much needed shadow work, I'm much more approachable. My issue was trust, I still didn't trust men because I still had a fear of them lurking in the shadows of my mind and I think they picked up on that.

I really had to do some meditation and shadow work to change that energy around (removing my resting bitch face helped as well).

I was being approached a little more because some men would see who they find attractive and shoot their shot, but I still wasn't letting anyone close to me. I was still the incredibly shrinking violet when faced with a room full of the opposite sex.

Got time for a couple of stories?

There was an owner of a repair company that I hired to do a job for me in my home and he was attractive, so we became flirty with one another for the duration of his job. I hired him for a couple of jobs and after a while, we began to talk sociably. One day he came over, one thing led to another, and he started to become touchy-feely which I absolutely consented to. A little way into the make-out session, I noticed I couldn't feel him touching me. I'm not talking figuratively; I mean I physically could not feel his hands on me. I started to feel disconnected from my body and so I stopped him abruptly. He left and I started running my hands up and down my body, trying to see if I could feel my own touch, which after a few minutes, I could. I had no idea why that happened, and I just attributed it to my body's reaction that he might be a sleazeball and I unconsciously didn't want him to be the one to test out my new body. Turned out, he was indeed a sleazeball and had a significant other.

I want to point out that I disclose everything upfront with any potential partner, I discuss my sexual trauma, and weight loss journey which includes my skin issues, prior to us getting to the point of intimacy. One of my friends asked why I do this, and I feel that I need to know what kind of man he is, and he needs to know what he may have to deal with. Of course, I don't bring all of this up on a first date. I disclose as time or situations occur. For example, men only see me with my clothes on either in person or in photos on my dating profiles. If I am talking to a guy and he repeatedly comments on how "fine" I look and how much I must work out to keep fit. I know that is a sign that he is very interested in a physically fit and aesthetically pleasing body.

I can cover up the skin fully clothed, but he is going to see the real deal if I wear a tank top or a certain type of jeans without a long shirt. Plus, if we were to get to the point of intimacy, not only would he feel it through my clothes, but he would see it once I am undressed. A lot of men might be turned off by that or feel like I wasn't being honest upfront about what I really look like, which would be devastating. I don't wish to see that type of disappointment or disgust on someone's face.

Another reason for full disclosure is that some men don't want a former big girl because their fear is that the weight will return either when they have a baby, as they get older, or just plain fall off the Fit Wagon. They are not attracted to big women and don't want to get involved with one that may tend to return to being overweight. Either way, I am not mad at them for their preference as I too, have certain preferences when choosing a partner, therefore I am completely honest so I can vet out the ones that are not for me. I am also confident that there are men out there who won't mind taking the journey with me.

Okay, let's try this again, shall we?

Fast-forward to another gentleman, who was older than me, and he applauded my weight loss efforts, wasn't turned off by the thought of loose skin, and was very calm and confident which I guess made me feel more comfortable because we did end up being intimate. There was still one problem, I had to drink to get myself relaxed enough to perform. I don't mean a glass of wine or two, which gets me tipsy because my body handles liquor differently with the surgery, so a glass or two can knock me down. I would take a few shots which inebriated me and then I would become someone else. Someone else who was enjoying herself but not really present with what was happening. Someone who was performing well and doing and saying all the right things but felt nothing. This relationship didn't last long; however, I am grateful for it because it uncovered a piece of the puzzle that I needed to explore. But the great news is, I finally had a relationship that ended amicably, and we are friends to this day.

As a matter of fact, alcohol, for a while, became my go-to since food wasn't an option. I am not one of those people who began to overeat emotionally and thus gain all the weight back. I am one of those people now who will not eat when I'm emotionally stressed or experiencing something traumatic resulting in rapid weight loss. I turned to alcohol heavily during 2020 when the world stood still. I moved in with my bestie Adriane during the fall of 2019 because I was being evicted from my rental as the owner decided to move back into her home from Denver. I was told this wonderful bit of news while overseas with the statement that I needed to be out in 30 days. I called Adriane from Morocco crying uncontrollably and she, ever the Virgo, advised me to enjoy my trip, do not think about this another minute as I would move in with her. I called my brother and

TRANSFORMED

I said he would be fine as he would get his own place and moving in with Adriane was what I needed.

I was only supposed to stay there until I got another job in the UK, California, or Canada which is where I wanted to go after graduating in December. Then the world shut down from COVID-19 and I, for the first time, had a chance to grieve the loss of my grandmother, my uncle, and my house. It was so heavy to deal with emotionally, so I turned to drinking. I felt I had lost the makeshift family that I created in one swoop. I am a natural caregiver without anyone to care for. I had paid off all my debt but that left me with nothing and a piss poor credit score. I was a small size but what was that doing for me? For my life? I was still unhappy. AB (which is what I affectionately call her) was the one to point out that I was downing a gallon of wine every couple of days, plus hard liquor. I would have my drinks at night to help me sleep without dreaming.

After being called out, I started to slow down on the drinks and started turning my attention to her cat. Mind you up until that point, I was terrified and reviled by these creatures. But I think I needed something to focus my love and attention on. I also had her daughter there as well, so she was totally included in the love and affection. But I began to take care of Bella like she was my own (I thought I only loved her and not cats in general until a few years later my own Sebastian showed up on my doorstep and I took him in).

TRANSFORMED

I wound up staying with Adriane for two years, and it was a time of complete transformation for me. She, Bella, and my niece, Camryn loved me back to life as I didn't realize how wounded I was from the past. Plus, she literally aided in whipping me into shape, physically (she's a fitness competitor) and financially.

Quick story:

A year before the pandemic, I was already at goal weight. Adriane and I had gone out to dinner, on the return trip home, she mentioned that I should have been working out this entire time like the doctor suggested and she suggested I focus more than just cardio exercises. I know I was just skin and bones without any muscle mass. She asked me if I ever looked at my arms as they have zero definition. I said that I look at my body every day, so yes, I know what my arms look like. Apparently, she wanted to make sure I saw what she saw. While I was driving, I saw her quietly taking a picture of my arms from the side! I was like, is she seriously trying to sneak a picture??? She looked at me and said she wanted to make sure that I knew exactly what my arms looked like. Freaking Virgo.

So, I think because I was being held hostage at her house during the pandemic, she recruited me to be a part of her fit squad. She came into my room one day and asked me what time I log off daily and I told her 4 pm. She stated, "Be downstairs in workout gear at 4:30

pm." She didn't ask me…. she told me. But it was the best thing she could've done, and I have been working out with the squad since that day.

I got back on track spiritually and in doing so started having dreams and visitations from my ancestors, spirit guides, and others (I will save the details for another book if given the green light by God/Goddess to share my full spiritual journey) which led me to completely turn around my finances. By August of 2021, I had a pretty decent credit score, a new car, a new place, and a potential new lover.

One more story for the road…

I wound up getting involved with a younger man who, strangely enough, made me feel the same level of comfort as the older gentleman. At first, I was reluctant to even entertain a younger man because, of course, first, he is used to younger bodies. Second, probably has zero experience dealing with trauma, and third, what did we really have in common? Turns out, we had so much in common and he brought a fresh millennial perspective on a lot of topics. He also was so passionate about everything and could discuss anything. Even when I told him about my weight loss and the trepidation I had with my skin, he was unfazed. During our time of being intimate, I realized I was still drinking to perform, but as time went on and we began to have sleepovers; put it this way, I wasn't going to have a cocktail for breakfast.

My slow aha moment was that I needed time, trust, and an emotional and mental connection with my partner to be comfortable enough to stay present and engaged in a sexual experience. I probably will not ever be that person who can have random encounters as I am not wired that way because of what has happened to me. I can accept that. I'm grateful to know that I am not damaged to the extent that I would never be able to enjoy intimacy with a partner without being under the influence.

This experience was designed to show me what was possible in my forever relationship, that I was ready and equipped to enter a long-term relationship and marriage. I was able to understand that in order to stop attracting emotionally unavailable men, I had to be emotionally present for myself. I had to show up being the very best, authentic version of myself and advocate for what I wanted, in order to attract the partner who would complement me in a union.

This encounter, although a wonderful experience, did eventually come to an end, but it wasn't destined to last. Remember that every experience with a partner isn't designed to be the be-all-end-all but is there to teach you about yourself and assist in your elevation to the next level.

While all of this was happening, I was able to do freelance work as a writer! Woohoo! So, I was saving my coins because I was determined to start phase one of my body lift. During the summer of 2022, I was able to secure the funds to schedule my first round of cosmetic surgery which I did on November 23rd.

Here we go...

CHAPTER 9

Every Ending Is A New Beginning

The time was finally here that I was going to have the first phase of what I personally call "The Reconstruction and Cleanup" phase of my "Build a Baddie" program. I did my due diligence and chose my cosmetic surgeon because I saw her previous work and she was accustomed to performing lifts after excessive weight loss. She understood how to get the optimal results with my body type being a woman of color, plus she was award-winning with her breast augmentation.

Because this was a cosmetic procedure, I couldn't take short-term disability, so I scheduled my surgery around a holiday, specifically Thanksgiving so that the company holidays were built in with a weekend, and then I took a few additional days off. I was new to my company, so I wasn't working with a large amount of PTO, therefore I had to be strategic.

Again, this is another instance where you are going to need a great hands-on support system. I didn't have my mom present for this surgery so my entire sister circle, my brother, and nieces all pitched in and took shifts during my recovery. If you don't have people in your life for aftercare, please save enough money to pay to stay at a recovery house. My surgery went picture perfect, but the pain afterward was excruciating, and I needed so much help, walking, dealing with my drains, and bathing. You also need transportation for your office check-ups and massages, which are quite often in the first three months.

I had only two complications, but it wasn't during the medical procedure. After about the third day, I began to have sharp head pain and I wasn't moving my bowels. Turns out I was having an allergic reaction to the codeine I was prescribed. I had to stop using the painkillers so from that point I felt every bit of the pain during recovery. I liken it to the vampire movie, where the girl was turning, and from the outside, she was stark still but inside she was in hell. I was that girl. Having to recover from having skin removed from my abdomen, arms, and breasts plus implants without pain medication was so traumatic for my body and psyche. I decided right after that I would have to wait about two years before I undergo phase two.

Another complication was my left arm swelling up considerably which caused my entire side to go numb and change coloring. I called the doctor and told her what was happening, and she advised me to remove my compression garment immediately. This allowed some of the swelling to subside, however, that side of my body took a very long time to return to normal and the left breast was still in a very slow drop and fluff stage. Drop and Fluff is what they call the implant settling into the proper position and softening.

I can see clearly now the skin is gone...

I have been working out faithfully with Adriane and the crew since 2020. My sister circle always encouraged me to keep at it so that the remaining skin after my skin removal procedure would wrap nicely around my newly built muscle. So, I kept at it, even though I was initially against strength training with weights because I didn't want to look like a muscle woman or a man. I said the same thing every time they had me go up in weight until one day, Adriane threatened to knock my ass out with the very dumbbell she was instructing me to use. Even though I couldn't really see the fruits of my labor, I continued to work out and build muscle. Once I began to heal from the surgery, I understood the method to their madness. I had a definition on my arms, and I could see it in my abdomen. Great Scott, they were right! So, I am focusing on my lower body to prepare for the next phase.

PSA: Please do not wait to start strength training after you lose weight as it is very hard to build up the muscle you have lost, especially if it's a significant amount of weight. You are losing both fat and muscle rapidly. Start with weights as soon as you are cleared by your medical team.

I would also, if you can afford it, pay for a personal trainer. I just happened to have fitness trainers and competitors within my circle, so I had a lot of people preparing workout routines, guiding my workouts, and correcting my form along the way. I see far too many people in the gym who don't know what they are doing, and they are not yielding results and could possibly injure themselves.

The After Party:

Life is pretty damn good, and it continues to get better. It's a completely different life from the one I had just eight years ago. Scientists say that your cells regenerate completely every seven years, and I am in alignment with my transformation in so many ways. I am loving my new body! I see how my hard work paid off and the goddess I envisioned and fantasized about for so many years is in the flesh. Sometimes, I look in the mirror in disbelief that this woman is staring back at me. My bestie Adriane asked me when I first started this journey if I wanted to chronicle it via video and I adamantly told her no. In retrospect, maybe I should have but I had failed in my attempts so many times that I didn't think I could've survived yet another failure. The thing I committed to most was taking photos. Seeing my own success proved to me that I could do anything and be fearless. Never again be afraid to do anything you want to and chronicle it because trying is never a failure, failing to try is. I have a whole new perspective on me.

I know who I am, and I love Her.

I approach life differently. Now, I am more unapologetic and more relentless in my quest for my bliss. Does it often translate into something that's not so nice? Sometimes, you can't make an omelet without breaking eggs. There are times when being a hero for yourself you might have to be a villain to others.

I'm more in tune with nature and the world around me. I meditate more, and I'm more aligned with spiritual practices that I've chosen, not religious beliefs that were placed upon me, due to tradition and the family I was born in. I tell people now that I have spiritual practices, not religious beliefs and that works for me. God/Goddess and I are cool.

I'm creating again, I'm writing again. I have a desire to create, and I think that's very important. Because I lost that for a long time, I couldn't write a single damn thing, I couldn't write a haiku If you asked me to. Shit, I couldn't write directions, if you asked me where

I was going. I'm looking forward to satisfying that personal journey as well in the near future.

Now, remember a few chapters back, when I had that monumental spiritual experience with God/Goddess, and they advised me that I had a mission? Well, now I know what it is:

This. Right. Here.

I had to go through these many life-altering traumas and trials not for shits and giggles, but because of what I represent for my family lineage and what I needed to impart to the world. I am my family's custodian, that was sent here to clear a lot of Karma and break generational curses. I am also called to put my story out to help anyone who may have been through similar situations and for them to know they are not alone and that they can make it to the other side. I'm not just talking about weight loss, I'm talking about molestation, sexual assault, spiritual disconnection, poverty, and the many symptoms that will result from these traumas.

This is why, even after receiving my bachelor's degree for my personal edification, I decided to become a Master Certified Life Coach, so I can help as many people as I can as this is my life's purpose. I'm living life, and that is a big difference from eight years ago. Five years ago, I was existing and requesting to make a hasty exit, now I am living and I'm literally requesting to be immortal, so that's how different life is right now, and I am just getting started. Remember that bridge I built and started to cross? I have now crossed it and burned it behind me. That old life serves no purpose for me, and I am co-creating the life I've always wanted, so I want to help others do the same thing for their lives.

Transformation.

It's so amazing that one decision can change your whole life, one moment, one thought can change the trajectory of your path. People don't understand that there are no small decisions because one little thing can literally lead you to a whole different timeline. I'm not even talking about me making the decision to have the weight loss surgery because that was major, but me just making the decision in my head that I needed to change, me literally waking up that night and realizing I was truly uncomfortable being fat and I needed to do something because this road wasn't going to work for me any longer. That decision to even start that process is what changed my entire life.

It's time to move.

You've been living in a hell cocoon long enough...break out!

My advice for the people thinking about getting weight loss surgery is: Do what's best for you, not what you feel is best for other people.

This is your life. I tell people all the time, you get one ride on this ride, no one gets the BOLO. Don't let anybody live your life for you, it's a waste of time, they get to live their lives and make their decisions just like you get to live your life and make yours. I know everything happens for a reason, so I try not to live in "I wish I could have" moments, but sometimes I do regret not doing the surgery sooner, however, I'd like to think that if I had done it sooner, I may not have gotten a chance to work with the medical team that I did. So, it all happened and played out the way it was supposed to play out. Do your research. Prepare yourself mentally. Get your core circle for support because you will need it.

Weight loss surgery gets a bad rap sometimes as an easy way out, and people are ashamed to do it, there's no shame in it at all. Again, like I said at the very beginning of the book, there's more than one way to get to ten. This was my way to get to ten. This might be your way to get to ten or it might be something else, but for those who are seriously thinking about it, there is a wonderful, beautiful life on the other side, you just must literally, without sounding cliche, trust the process and dedicate yourself to the process. Don't half-ass anything. If you're going to do it, go all in, balls to the wall, because it does work. It will work. Will it be a lot of work? Yes, but the final result is worth it.

For those who have decided to do it, I have laid some of the stuff out ahead for you, hopefully, your road is even smoother than mine. But just know that this is not a magic wand that is going to miraculously fix every aspect of your life, you must do that work as well. The physical part is just part of the work, there's spiritual work, there's the mental and emotional work that comes along with all the changes that are going to happen to you physically, and that will manifest out emotionally and mentally, and they'll also permeate those around you. So, make sure that you have a core group of people that you know got your back, and that is your group that's gonna ride for you because unfortunately or fortunately, as you change, people around you may change. You must be prepared for that. Be unapologetic in your quest for your bliss, be relentless in your quest for your bliss. Don't let anybody tell you differently. Don't allow anybody to shame you into changing your mind or rethinking things or pushing it back to see if you can try a natural weight loss thing, one more time, if you feel like this is what resonates with you, you tell those people that...they can go ahead and eat a fat stack of pancakes, because this is not their life, this is yours, and this journey is what you make out of it, life is what you make out of it. And if this is what you need to do, you need to do it.

To the Support Team:

For those people who have someone around them who is contemplating taking this route or has even made the decision, don't judge them based on what you have done, what you can do, or what you're doing. Everyone's body is different. Everyone's journey is different, everybody's life is different. What you can do is be there for that person, assist them in any way you can, support and encourage them. That's what they need. That's what everyone really needs to achieve any type of goal or major transformation. They don't need judgment, they don't need condescension, and they don't need naysayers. If you can't do this, take a back seat, and let somebody else to the forefront who can, because it can be an incredible but difficult process.

Dust Yourself off and try again...

For those people who are reading this book and had weight loss surgery, lost weight, and then gained all that shit back, I see you. No judgment here, I've been where you've been. We've all been where you've been. I can tell you that it's not too late, but you need to suck it up buttercup. Pull yourself up by your bootstraps and make that tool work for you again. Once we're given the tool, we always have it.

TRANSFORMED

Is it gonna be a little bit harder this time than it was the first time? Abso-fuckin-lutely. But it also will be worth it because you came out on the other side at one point and had reached your goal weight or had gotten down significantly and felt great about yourself, now if you are fine the way you are, cool. But if you're unhappy, you still have that tool, you need to dust that bitch off and get to work, get your support system back in place or get a new squad if you need to, pull out your guidelines, get a workout schedule in place and get to work. You know what it takes and what to do…you just require an encore performance.

There's light at the end of this tunnel.

For all those who may have suffered from physical, emotional, or mental trauma. I understand what that's like, to be violated in that way. While I know the experiences have forever changed me but not forever damaged or controlled me. Going to therapy was the best decision I was ever "required" to make. It will truly help you put the pieces back together and you will walk in the light again. There is healing in the light. They don't win.

Unleashed on the World!

Remember when I said, "If I could just help one person achieve their goal, it was worth it." To hell with that shit! I want to change the world and help thousands, no, millions of people find their bliss, because I know everybody deserves and is worthy of living their best life.

No one deserves to exist and then die; everyone deserves to live. This is why I'm putting it all out there so that as many people as possible can read my story, benefit from my journey, embark on their own journeys, turn around, and pass that along to the next person.

This is what it's going to take to change the world and create a better present. You must be the change for someone else to see that change is possible.

Know that someone cares and is with you on your journey in spirit. I want you to go back to the different parts of this book that you resonate with, that help light that flame…that gives you the motivation to do what you need to do to live the best life you envision for yourself, no matter what that is for you.

Know that I truly see you.
I am here with you.
I understand you.
I love you.
Ase'
Let us begin…

ABOUT THE AUTHOR

Nia Danielle, originally from Newark, NJ, showed an early passion for books, captivating family members with her precocious memory and love for storytelling. When she was just two years old, she had her family members convinced that she knew how to read, when in fact, she was memorizing verbatim the books being read to her and would recite them along with knowing when exactly to turn each page.

She honed her creative talents through poetry, short stories, and performances in drama and chorus throughout her schooling. After graduating from The Art Institute of Atlanta with a degree in video production, Nia embarked on a successful career in media, as head of post-production for home improvement shows which aired on HGTV, including writing, producing, and directing independent projects in the Atlanta area. Following a hiatus, she returned to academia, earning a Bachelor of Fine Arts degree in Motion Pictures and Television from the Academy of Art University, alongside certification as a Master Life Coach. With a wealth of experience in media and a newfound dedication to empowering others, Nia is thrilled to debut her first book and ready to inspire readers on their transformative journeys.

www.ingramcontent.com/pod-product-compliance
Lightning Source LLC
Chambersburg PA
CBHW072128160426
43197CB00012B/2029